Everything you always wanted to know about

PROPHECY

but didn't know who to ask!

by
Dr. Jack Van Impe

Second Printing, 1981
Third Printing, 1983
Fourth Printing, 1986
Fifth Printing, 1989
Sixth Printing, 1991
Revised, 1993
Revised, Second Printing, 1993

Jack Van Impe Ministries
P.O. Box 7004, Troy, Michigan 48007
In Canada: Box 1717, Postal Station A
Windsor, Ontario N91 6YA

ISBN 0-934803-11-0

Contents

Contents

Introduction

Introduction

There is great confusion today about Bible prophecy. For that reason, it is my desire to clarify questions about Bible prophecy from the truths I have learned during many thousands of hours of Bible study. I believe Jesus intended us to study the prophetic scriptures, for according to 2 Timothy 4:7,8, one of the five crowns presented to the children of God is for faithfully studying prophecy and looking for His coming.

The questions contained in this text have been compiled from the many, many questions received from friends throughout the U.S., Canada, and the world. These questions represent some of the most commonly asked and most puzzling queries men and women have today concerning end-time prophetic scriptures.

It is my prayer that the information contained in this book will help each reader prepare for Christ's return, and will challenge Christians everywhere—regardless of how long they have known Jesus as Saviour and Lord—to live a life of commitment, holiness, and service.

1

Israel and Bible Prophecy

What is Bible prophecy?

It is history written in advance—God's description of future events.

Can prophecy be trusted?

Yes. God is omniscient and knows all things. Acts 15:18 says, *Known unto God are all his works from the beginning of the world.* The term *omniscient* means God knows everything about everything, and all things about all things. Therefore, because He can see the future—being omniscient—He can tell us what will happen 100, 1,000, 5,000, even 50,000 years in advance, and—no matter how much time elapses—even the most minute detail will happen *exactly like it was prophesied, because God said it!*

Is Bible prophecy always accurate?

Definitely! The scriptures were actually statements made by the all-knowing God through earthly vessels. *Holy men of God spake as they were moved by the Holy Ghost* (2 Peter 1:21). There are hundreds of prophecies about Christ's first and second coming in the Bible. The law of compound probabilities tells us that the posibility or chance of each one of these being fulfilled is about one in a billion. And God's Word has not failed, even in one small detail, concerning Christ's first coming.

In fact, it stated that He would be the seed of woman (Genesis 3:15); He would come through the line of Abraham, Isaac, and Jacob (Genesis 12:3,17-19); He would be a descendant of Judah (Genesis 49:10); He would be born in Bethlehem (Micah 5:2); He would be born of a virgin—the precious virgin Mary, untouched by a man (Isaiah 7:14); He would sojourn into Egypt (Hosea 11:1); and He would grow up at Nazareth and be called a Nazarene (Matthew 2:23).

The Bible also stated that He would grow to manhood and be crucified (Psalm 22:14-16). These verses were written 500 years before the Romans instituted crucifixion as a form of execution!

Finally, the Bible stated that He would be raised from the dead (Job 19:25). These and many other Old Testament prophecies foretold what would happen to Jesus in the New Testament. And every one of these prophecies occurred down to the smallest detail, with perfection, and without exception. As Christ came the first time, He will come again (Acts 1:11). I personally believe His return will be very, very soon!

What is the difference between a prophet and a prognosticator?

A prophet has been shown the order of future events by God himself. *Surely the Lord God...revealeth his secret unto his servants the prophets* (Amos 3:7). Prognosticators usually *guess* what is going to happen, and sometimes are correct. Others become involved with the spirit world and, when their predictions come true, it is because of demonic influence. Leviticus 19:31 tells us, *Regard not them that have familiar spirits, neither seek after wizards, to be defiled by them: I am the Lord your God.*

Why is there so little teaching today about prophetic events or what the Bible says about the future?

Primarily because it demands so much study and research. Many do not want to spend the time necessary to study the prophetic scriptures and dig into God's Word as they should. The Bible says, *Study to show thyself approved unto God, a workman that needeth not to be ashamed, rightly dividing the word of truth* (2 Timothy 2:15).

Secondly, many men do not teach from the prophetic scriptures because they are afraid of being branded as "sensationalists." This is sad, because the message of Christ's return is a *blessed hope* (Titus 2:13), a purifying hope (see 1 John 3:2,3), and a hope that earns one a special crown (see 2 Timothy 4:7,8).

But Jesus was a sensationalist! And much of what He said was also sensational. For instance: *For as the lightning cometh out of the east, and shineth even unto the west; so shall also the coming of the Son of man be* (Matthew 24:27); *Immediately after the tribulation of those days shall the sun be darkened, and the moon shall not give her light, and the stars shall fall from heaven* (Matthew 24:29). Jesus made these shocking statements! So we are branded as sensationalists, like Jesus, when we preach the Word of God.

Can the Book of Revelation be understood?

The Book of Revelation was given to *reveal* the truth, not *conceal* it, and to *clarify* God's eternal purpose, not *mystify* it.

Can prophecy itself truly be understood?

Yes. The Bible says, *Blessed is he that readeth, and they that hear the words of this prophecy, and keep those things which are written therein: for the time is at hand* (Revelation 1:3). God would not promise a special blessing to those who read, hear, and keep the words of prophecy if it were impossible to understand them.

Why do some people prefer not to hear teaching on prophetic events?

Because of worldliness, men don't want to hear about prophetic events. First John 2:15-17 says, *Love not the world, neither the things that are in the world. If any man love the world, the love of the Father is not in him. For all that is in the world, the lust of the flesh, and the lust of the eyes, and the pride of life, is not of the Father, but is of the world. And the world passeth away, and the lust thereof.* The message of Christ's return is a "purifying hope" (see 1 John 3:2,3). This is the sort of hope that makes a person holy if he really believes it. For these reasons, men don't preach it, and many don't even want to hear it.

In 1948 Israel became a nation. Is this the fulfillment of Matthew 24:32, which speaks of the fig tree blossoming?

No doubt about it! When Israel became a nation—May 14, 1948—that's when the fig tree blossomed! How do I know that Israel is the fig tree? The law of first mention. When anything is mentioned the first time in Scripture, it becomes that throughout God's Word. For instance, Joel 1:7 tells us that when the enemy armies were invading Israel, *He hath laid my vine waste, and barked my fig tree* [Israel]. Then, of course, Hosea 9:10 says, *I saw your fathers as the firstripe in the fig tree.* Here,

11

again, God is speaking to Jews. Thus, the fig tree is Israel.

Will there ever be a time when Jews will be converted on a worldwide basis?

Yes—when Christ comes (see Revelation 19) and sets His foot *upon the mount of Olives* (Zechariah 14:4), all the tribes of the earth [which means the twelve tribes of Israel] will mourn. Romans 11:26 says, *All Israel shall be saved.* Why? Because *there shall come out of Sion the Deliverer, and shall turn away ungodliness from Jacob.*

A total of 144,000 Jews will preach the gospel of the kingdom during the Tribulation hour. Then, when Russia invades the Middle East and God performs one of His greatest miracles on behalf of the Israelites (see Ezekiel 39:22), their eyes will be opened. Thus, somewhere toward the end of the Armageddon period—or as Christ returns to judge the nations (Matthew 25:31-46)—a tremendous nationwide conversion of God's people, the Jews, takes place.

There is no doubt about it. Jews are going to be saved *en masse.* The greatest hour in history is coming for Israel!

Will the fulfillment of this promise involve a lengthy period of time?

No. Israel will be born in one day. *And it shall come to pass in that day, that I will seek to*

12

destroy all the nations that come against Jerusalem. And I will pour upon the house of David, and upon the inhabitants of Jerusalem, the spirit of grace and of supplications: and they shall look upon me whom they have pierced, and they shall mourn for him (Zechariah 12:9,10). Zechariah 13:1 says, *In that day there shall be a fountain opened to the house of David and to the inhabitants of Jerusalem for sin and for uncleanness.*

Is there an outline in the Bible that we can go by—past, present, and future—as far as the Jews are concerned?

Yes! Romans 9, 10, and 11. Chapter 9 tells of the Jews' past and describes their heritage (verses 1-5). Chapter 10:1-3 tells of their present blindness in rejecting the Messiah. Chapter 11 describes their coming blessing, when *all Israel shall be saved* (Romans 11:26). What a glorious future!

Some people believe that Christians—believers—are the true Israelites. How do you feel about that?

That's where we get into trouble! The text used by these proponents is Romans 2:28,29: *For he is not a Jew, which is one outwardly* [in the flesh]...*but he is a Jew, which is one inwardly.* But this is not accurate in the light of Galatians 3:28, which tells us that there is *neither Jew nor Greek* in Christianity...*neither bond nor free...neither male nor female.* Literally taken, that would make transvestites out of all of us. Likewise, God does not change Christians into spiritual Israelites.

One can't do that! And here's why: the term *Israel* or *Israelite* is found 2,300 times in the Old Testament, and it is always in reference to Jacob, and Jacob becomes Israel (see 2 Kings 17:34).

Furthermore, Jacob and Israel are referred to as Jews eighty times in the Old Testament and 170 times in the New Testament. So how is one going to justify such overwhelming evidence? When Galatians 6:15,16 speaks about the God of Israel, it is in relation to converted Jews—Hebrew Christians. But that doesn't make the entire Church Jewish!

This one misconception has caused more damage to the cause of prophecy in our day than any other teaching! The theory started with Augustine in about 190 A.D., and has led to endless symbolizing, with many others following his error. That's where the confusion began. One can't justify it. Israel is Israel—period!

There are some who believe that the ten lost tribes of Israel are actually England and America. Is this true?

That's the theory known as *British Israelism*, propagated by Garner Ted Armstrong and his father, on their television program and in their magazine.

No, it isn't correct, because the names of the twelve tribes of Israel are found in Revelation 7:4-8—Juda, Reuben, Gad, Aser, Nephthalim, Manasses, Simeon, Levi, Issachar, Zabulon, Joseph, and Benjamin. And that doesn't sound like "Sherlock Holmes" or "Winston Churchill" (British names) to me!

A highway has just been built from the Far East to the Middle East. Is there any significance in this event, as far as Bible prophecy is concerned?

Definitely. The oriental armies are going to march across that highway on their trek down to the Middle East (see Revelation 16:12; Daniel 11:44).

In Matthew 24:34, Jesus says, *This generation shall not pass, till all these things be fulfilled.* **What exactly does "this generation" mean?**

There are those who say that *genea* is a term for "race"—"This race of Jews shall never pass away." These people believe that the Jews shall never pass until all the signs are fulfilled. That is true, for throughout history God has protected the people of Israel. But I believe it also means that the generation that lives to see all these prophetic events transpire shall not pass

15

from the earth until all the signs are completed. I further believe that *we are that generation!*

How long is a generation?

Oh, I love this! Matthew 1:17 tells us that *all the generations from Abraham to David are fourteen generations; and* [all the generations] *from David until the carrying away into Babylon are fourteen generations; and* [all the generations] *from the carrying away into Babylon unto Christ are fourteen generations.* When we add fourteen plus fourteen plus fourteen, the total is forty-two generations from Abraham to Christ.

The great chronologist, Thiele, says that from Abraham to Christ, we have a total of 2,160 years. Divide forty-two generations into that, and the length of a generation becomes 51.4. Add that to May 14, 1948, and one comes out at Rosh Hashanah, September 1999, when this generation that lives to see "all these things" comes to a glorious conclusion. We're not setting dates, but one has to admit—it's interesting!

There are many who feel that the 1990s could be the closing of this age of grace. Why?

The Bible says, *When ye shall see all these things, know that it* [the coming of Christ] *is near, even at the doors* (Matthew 24:33). When one sees the European Economic Community (the revived Roman Empire) forming and present situations developing in Russia and the mid-east, one knows that the time is near. All signs are already casting their shadow—or beginning to occur—simultaneously. Therefore, I believe the present generation could see Jesus Christ when He comes *in the twinkling of an eye.*

What exactly is meant by "the times of the Gentiles?"

It means Gentile dominion over the Jews and the world, or the period of Jewish captivity—beginning with the Babylonians and ending with Armageddon at the conclusion of the Tribulation hour. That period of Jewish captivity started under Nebuchadnezzar in 536 B.C. and extends until Armageddon.

Since Jerusalem is now under Jewish control, does this indicate that "the times of the Gentiles" is fulfilled?

No. Events which have occurred since the six-day war in 1967 prove that Israel's present possession of Jerusalem is temporary. The hordes out of the north will attempt to capture Jerusalem as they come against Israel (see Ezekiel 38:15,16). Therefore, one might see the control of the city shifting back and forth once or twice before the final onslaught. Once Armageddon occurs, however, Jerusalem will be controlled by the Jews forever.

We are approximately at that period when the *"times of the Gentiles"* is fulfilled, for Luke 21:24 says, *Jerusalem shall be trodden down of the Gentiles.* It was under Nebuchadnezzar that this domination began and it was not until June 1967 that the Jews again took Jerusalem. The Gentiles will try to get it back when *all nations* [are gathered] *against Jerusalem to battle* (Zechariah 14:2), and will capture the city briefly. Then Messiah will appear and destroy the armies of the world (see Zechariah 14:4). Immediately the times of the Gentiles will cease.

When was Jerusalem first mentioned in the Bible?
Genesis 14:18 speaks of the city of *Salem* over which Melchizedek was king. Later the term *Jehru* was used. When the two were combined, the name became *Jerusalem,* and has been known as such for over 4,000 years.

Is there any significance to Jerusalem being rebuilt in our generation?
Definitely! Jerusalem is going to be the capital of the world! The very fact that the Jews are now in control of Jerusalem—and have been since the six-day war of 1967—proves that the times of the Gentiles is coming to a swift conclusion and that Jesus must come very soon.

When will the Jews resume worship in their Temple, actually offering sacrifices again, as prophesied in the Bible?

There could, in fact, be two temples—one desecrated by the Antichrist as he sits there calling himself God (2 Thessalonians 2:4), building an image of himself to be worshiped (Revelation 13:15), and another after the seven years of Tribulation. I am not certain whether there will be one temple which will be cleansed after having been defiled by the Antichrist, or whether an entirely new temple will be constructed after the Tribulation. Regardless of whether there will be one or two temples, we find the Jews offering sacrifices once again in the Temple, in Ezekiel 40 through 48.

The Jews from throughout the world are returning to Israel. Yet the largest number of Jews yet dispersed anywhere in the globe is in the United States. Will there be a great exodus of Jews from the United States to Israel?

Ezekiel 36:24, Amos 9:15, and other portions of Scripture indicate that the Jews will return to their homeland from all over the world. According to Jeremiah 3:17,18, the last group to return home will be from the north—Russia. We're seeing it happen now. However, I don't think there will be a mass exodus, as far as America is concerned, until Christ returns.

Matthew 24:31, which is the introduction to the Millennium, says that when Christ comes to reign for a thousand years, the eighth trumpet sounds, and its blast causes all the elect from the four winds—north, south, east, and west—to return. That's when I believe Jews from the U.S. will migrate *en masse* to Israel.

Does the "gospel of the kingdom," preached by the 144,000 Jews (Revelation 7:4-8), include the blood of Jesus Christ?

Yes—they're going to be preaching the same message that John the Baptist preached—the message that the King is coming (Matthew 24:14). John's message also included repentance (Matthew 3:2) and the blood, for he said, *Behold the Lamb of God, which taketh away the sin of the world* (John 1:29). How did He take away the sin of the world? By the shedding of His blood (see Ephesians 1:7). By inspiration of the Holy Spirit, the Apostle John wrote in Revelation 1:5, *Unto him that loved us, and washed us from our sins in his own blood.*

In every dispensation, there is only one way to get saved! That is by the blood, whether it was under Moses' law (past), whether it is under grace (present), or whether it is during the Tribulation hour (future). It is the blood of Jesus that makes *atonement for...souls* (Leviticus 17:11). *And without shedding of blood is no remission* [of sins] (Hebrews 9:22).

Thus, John, warning the people that the King was coming, preached repentance and the sacrifice of Christ. The 144,000 will promote the same message.

Who are the "elect" of Matthew 24:22?

Oh, I like this! The post-tribulationists use this verse—*Except those days should be shortened, there should no flesh be saved: but for the elect's sake those days shall be shortened*—saying it indicates that the Church will be here because we are the elect. I say, "Hold it! God has two elect groups on earth!"

There is the Church (see Ephesians 1:4; 1 Peter 1:2), but that is not the group referred to in Matthew 24:22. How do I know? Isaiah 42:1 speaks of the Jews as God's *elect*. So does Isaiah 45:4, 65:9, and 65:22. How does one know that the Jews are the elect for whom the days are being shortened in Matthew 24:22?

Let's keep the text in context. First of all, this elect group is to flee from Judaea to the mountains. Judaea, my friend, is the Holy Land (see Matthew 24:16)! They are not to flee on the *sabbath day* [shabbat] (Matthew 24:20). According to Exodus 31:13, the Sabbath Day is eternally practiced by the Jews. In Mark 13:9, we find that they are *beaten in the synagogues*...not the church. We don't meet in synagogues because we are the Church (see Acts 2:47).

Finally, all these events take place in the area of Jerusalem (see Luke 21:24). So the elect, at this point in time, are Jews—Israelites.

Who are the "two witnesses" mentioned in Revelation 11:3?

There are three persons from Bible history who most men will invariably choose as candidates for the *two witnesses* mentioned in Revelation 11:3—Moses, Elijah, and Enoch. I personally believe the two witnesses will be Moses and Elijah. Why? Because in Matthew 17, when Jesus took Peter, James, and John to the mount and was transfigured before them, it was Moses and Elijah who appeared with Him. At the transfiguration, Moses and Elijah appeared with Jesus—not Moses and Enoch, not Elijah and Enoch.

The transfiguration scene, then, is a picture of that coming day when the two witnesses—Moses and Elijah—will be revealed.

Malachi 4:5,6 predicts that Elijah will come as one of the two witnesses. This prediction is corroborated by the fact that Elijah did not die a physical death but was taken up into heaven by a whirlwind and chariot of fire (see 2 Kings 2:9-11). The Bible also tells us that Moses' body was preserved by God (see Deuteronomy 34:5,6; Jude 9). So these are good Bible reasons why I believe the two witnesses will be Moses and Elijah.

So much is now being written and spoken about the revived Roman Empire. What is the revived Roman Empire?

My video study, *Revelation Revealed, Verse by Verse,* presents a ten-hour, in-depth study on this subject. Here are a few glimpses: the ten toes (Daniel 2) and ten horns of the beast (Daniel 7) represent the ten nations that will unite together at the endtime to form the revived Roman Empire. These ten nations must be nations that were part of the original Roman Empire.

It all started with Belgium, Holland, Luxembourg (1948); then Italy, France, West Germany (1957); next, England, Ireland, and Denmark (1973). And finally, Greece (1981) was added to make ten nations. But the problem is that Denmark and Ireland do not belong, because they were not a part of the original Roman Empire. So there must be others coming in. That's why we presently see it as twelve nations, counting Portugal and Spain, because two are going out.

We could get into all the ramifications, but the point is, when there are exactly ten nations that were all part of the original Roman Empire, that is when Christ will return. When there are ten—the final ten, after all the changes have been made—then shall the God of heaven set up His kingdom. It shall never be destroyed. That's when He comes as *KING OF KINGS, AND LORD OF LORDS* (Revelation 19:16).

Has there ever been in history an alignment of nations like the one you just described?

No. This is the first time in world history that we have had nations aligning that were part of the old Roman Empire, which can now honestly be called the revived Roman Empire. And, unbelievable as it may seem, it was the Club of Rome in 1957 that approved this amalgamation of nations. Now their constitution is based on the Treaty of Rome. If you don't think this is the revived Roman Empire, what is? We call it the E.C.—the Economic Community. Watch it in the headlines in days to come!

Our President and world leaders everywhere have been talking about a New World Order. What is the New World Order?

This grouping—the revived Roman Empire, or E.C.—I believe, forms the foundation of the New World Order (see Daniel 7:20), out of which the Antichrist will arise (see Revelation 13:1). This beast (Antichrist) has all the world marveling and wondering after him, saying, *Who is like unto the beast?* Also, *Power was given him over all kindreds, and tongues, and nations. And all that dwell upon the earth shall worship him...And he causeth all, both small and great, rich and poor, free and bond, to receive a mark* (Revelation 13:4,7,8,16).

You have always said that Russia would march down from the north and invade Israel. Now, because communism has literally crumbled, has your opinion changed?

No. I have a full-length video on this topic. It's our best-seller, *Russia, World War III, and Armageddon*. For forty years I've preached this message across America to audiences totaling ten million people, and I have never spoken of a coming war with the U.S.S.R. (Union of Soviet Socialist Republics)! I always said, "Russia!"

So if the entire empire disintegrated, it still wouldn't matter, because it would be *Rosh*—the Hebrew word for "chief prince," which is *Rucia* in Greek, and *Russia* in English! The prophecy is still 100 percent correct!

Where does America fit into end-time prophecy?

Many great theologians, such as Dr. Logsden, former pastor of Moody Memorial Church, taught that Isaiah 18, Jeremiah 50-51, and Revelation 18, depicted America as Babylon. There are many tremendous reasons why these great men believed this.

For further enlightenment, I suggest that you study my video teaching, *America in Prophecy*.

What groups of people will compose the one-world church?

All of apostate Christendom (Revelation 17:4,5,9,15,18).

Since Revelation 20:4 says, *I saw the souls of them that were beheaded for the witness of Jesus, and for the word of God,* we have to believe that all those taken at the Rapture were those who believed that *all scripture* [was] *given by inspiration of God* (2 Timothy 3:16), that *holy men of God spake* [and wrote] *as they were moved by the Holy Ghost* (2 Peter 1:21); and that they believed everything the Bible had to say about Jesus.

That means they believed that Jesus was God from all eternity (Romans 9:5; 1 Timothy 3:16); that He was born of the precious virgin Mary (Matthew 1:23); that it was a miracle (Luke 1:35); that He *died for our sins* (1 Corinthians 15:3); that His blood was shed to cleanse all men from sin (1 John 1:7) [the shed blood is mentioned 700 times in the Bible!]; and that He rose bodily from the grave (1 Corinthians 15:3,4). This is the doctrine of Christ.

So all the churches remaining after the rapture of the Church will be those that denied the doctrine of Christ. *Who is a liar but he that denieth that Jesus is the Christ? He is antichrist* (1 John 2:22). May I say to multitudes within Christendom—watch out if you are in one of those churches denying these truths!

If one denies the doctrine of Christ is he upholding the doctrine of Antichrist?

Anyone who denies that Jesus is God is "anti-Christ." And these churches which band together to create the one-world church will center around the heretical teaching that deprecates or belittles Christ.

2

The Rapture and the Bride of Christ

What do you believe is the next event on God's prophetic time clock?

The Rapture.

What is the Rapture?

The term *rapture* comes from the Latin word, *rapio*, which means "a snatching away." The Rapture, then, is the time when the Lord comes in the clouds of glory, bodily (see Acts 1:11), to take out of this world—also bodily—all those who have died in Christ and who are still living as believers in the Saviour. First Thessalonians 4:16-18 describes it: *For the Lord himself shall descend from heaven with a shout, with the voice of the archangel, and with the trump of God, and the dead in Christ shall rise first: Then we which are alive and remain shall be caught up together with them* [the dead in Christ] *in the clouds, to meet the Lord in the air: and so shall we ever be with the Lord. Wherefore comfort one another with these words.*

We call it the Rapture because *rapio* means "a snatching away," in the Latin. The Rapture is described in 1 Corinthians 15:51: *I show you a mystery; We shall not all sleep* [be dead], *but we shall all be changed, in a moment, in the twinkling of an eye, at the last trump.* And so this *twinkling of an eye* is a "snatching away," and occurs as we zip through the heavenlies to meet Jesus Christ in clouds of glory.

First Corinthians 15:52 refers to the "last trump." The Book of Revelation also refers to the "last trump." Are they the same?

No. First Corinthians 15:51,52 is one scripture passage that post-Tribulationists (those who believe they are going to go through the Tribulation and will meet Christ at the end) use to defend that doctrine. *Behold, I show you a mystery; We shall not all sleep* [be dead], *but we shall all be changed. In a moment, in the twinkling of an eye, at the last trump.*

Then they go over to the trumpet judgments and say, "You see? The seventh trumpet [judgment] brings all this catastrophe, and this is right at the end of the Tribulation hour. And because He calls His church home at the last trump, it has to be at the end of the seven years of Tribulation."

Hold it! What about the eighth trump, when the trumpet sounds in Matthew 24:31 and He [gathers] *together his elect from the four winds* for the Millennium?

28

There's more by way of contradistinction. The seventh trump produces judgment and death, but the trumpet of 1 Corinthians 15:51 produces eternal life and joy, as believers sweep into the heavenlies to meet Him. That's when the dead and the living in Christ go to meet the Saviour in the twinkling of an eye.

How long is "the twinkling of an eye?"

Scientists at General Electric Company have measured the twinkling in a human being's eye, and it amounts to eleven one hundredths of a second. I hope the Rapture occurs some morning when the astronauts are on their way to Mars or some other planet. Suddenly the Lord says, *Come up hither* (Revelation 4:1). Immediately we zip through space—in the twinkling of an eye—right past the astronauts. I can see them trying to figure out what they're viewing from that altitude! "Houston, Houston...." UFOs? No. The coming of Jesus!

Presently the U.S. has two spacecraft exploring outer space. It is estimated that it will take 40,000 years to reach the first star and 120,000 years to reach the second star. Beyond that there are millions, billions, and even trillions of stars. However, when Christ says, *Come up hither,* we'll zip through millions of light years of space in eleven one hundredths of a second to see Jesus face to face.

A lot of people will be left behind when the Rapture occurs. How will the evacuation of so many people be explained to the people left behind?

A lot of folks write to this ministry, saying, "We are leaving all of your videos and books around, Dr. Van Impe, because when Jesus comes, we want people to find out exactly what happened to us!" So I'm sure there will be plenty of information available for those who really desire to know what happened to the ones taken in the Rapture.

However, there will also be a lot of *misinformation* available. The New Age movement has all kinds of books out on the market about beings they call the "space brothers." And New Agers are also talking about an evacuation of human beings in the near future. These New Agers are predicting a counterfeit experience around the year 2000. So there are many alternate theories to confuse people left behind.

Will there be a great revival, with many souls turning to God, before the Rapture?

God can do anything at any time. However, I do not think we'll experience a great revival before the Rapture, because 2 Timothy 3:13 states, *Evil men and seducers shall wax worse and worse, deceiving, and being deceived.*

Jesus also spoke about the latter day Church in Revelation 3:15: *I know thy works, that thou art neither cold nor hot: I would thou wert cold or hot. So then because thou art luke-warm, and neither cold nor hot, I will spue thee out of my mouth.* In this passage, Jesus said, "You make Me want to gurgitate because of your indifference, lackadaisicalness, and luke-warmness."

Presently some of our churches are so cold that we could have signs above the doors stating, **First Church of the Deep Freeze—Dr. Jack Frost, Pastor.**

However, there is going to be a great revival! When? During the seven-year Tribulation period, 144,000 Jews (see Revelation 7:4-8) will circle the globe, preaching the *gospel of the kingdom* (Matthew 24:14). *Gospel* means "good news." And this is the good news—the King is coming! At that time, the Bible says, *All Israel shall be saved* (Romans 11:26). That means the Jews! But when one gets to Revelation 7:9, it is a *great multitude.* And who are they? *These are they which came out of great tribulation, and have washed their robes, and made them white in the blood of the Lamb* (verse 14). They have trusted in the blood of the Lamb. They have been cleansed.

So we see both Jews and Gentiles saved for the greatest revival in history, because at that time, God says, *I will pour out my spirit upon all flesh* (Joel 2:28).

So the great revival is coming *after* the Rapture. Perhaps the Rapture will cause many

31

people to see that all these things they heard about Jesus and the Bible are true, so that they will want to know the Lord.

At the time of the Rapture, many Christian mothers will have unborn children within them, and there will be millions of little children on earth, also. Will all unborn babies be taken with their mothers, and will these millions of little children also be taken up in the Rapture?

Yes, definitely—because God is not an abortionist, and also because the Lord loves little children. The Bible makes this very clear. Every fetus within every mother who is taken up in the Rapture will also be taken up. Not only will the ones within wombs go, but so will all children who are under the age of accountability. Luke 18:16 says, *Suffer* [allow] *little children to come unto me, and forbid them not: for of such is the kingdom of God.* The Greek word *brephos* means "all little ones born and unborn." That means all the children who are under the age of accountability before God.

The Lord showed me something one day about children and the age of accountability. As I opened the pages of my Bible, the Holy Spirit showed this tremendous truth to me. Romans 5:19 says, *For as by one man's disobedience* [the sin of one man, Adam] *many were made sinners, so by the obedience of one* [Jesus] *shall many be made righteous.* Because of Christ's sacrifice on Calvary's cross, His righteousness—His free gift to mankind—came upon all men. So all are covered by the blood of Jesus, and His righteousness is bestowed upon all children until they come to the age where they can understand for themselves what the message of salvation is really about.

What is the age of accountability?

The age of accountability is not a specific age. It is not necessarily twelve or thirteen. In some cases, the age of accountability could be nine. The age of accountability can vary with each individual's upbringing and intellectual ability. When children know right from wrong and can either say, "I will follow the paths of righteousness by receiving Christ," or "I choose to reject it," they reach the age of accountability. Children are automatically covered until that time—whatever that age may be—or Romans 5:19 should not be in the Bible!

If a person has heard the gospel and rejected Jesus Christ, and the Rapture occurs, will that person have another opportunity to accept Jesus as Lord during the Tribulation?

Most evangelicals turn to 2 Thessalonians 2:11,12, which says, *And for this cause God shall send them strong delusion, that they should believe a lie: That they all might be damned who believed not the truth.* So the reasoning is that anyone who has ever heard the gospel and rejected it will not have a chance then.

I no longer believe that. Why?

As I was studying Acts 2:17, which repeats the prophetic passage of Joel 2:28, the Holy Spirit revealed something to me. God says, *I will pour out of my Spirit upon all flesh.* There is going to be enlightenment like never before—perhaps because the Rapture has already transpired. Then it hit me: This is in the *midst* of the Tribulation hour (see Acts 2:19-21)! This is in the midst of all judgment! That's when God says, *Whosoever shall call on the name of the Lord shall be saved* (Acts 2:21).

After an intensive study of Acts 2, I now believe that the only ones who are in that state of damnation, as outlined in 2 Thessalonians 2:12, are those who heard the gospel, and heard it, and heard it—and even then spurned it. That's why Romans 2:5 says, *But after thy hardness and impenitent heart treasurest up unto thyself wrath against the day of wrath.* So these individuals would literally be committing the unpardonable sin.

Could there be a partial Rapture?

No. There are those who teach that only the perfect will be taken in the Rapture, but this is contrary to the teaching of God's Word. Many base this teaching on Hebrews 9:28— *Unto them that look for him shall he appear the second time without sin unto salvation*—saying

34

that the Rapture is only for those who are looking for it. But that does not agree with the rest of the Bible. One cannot take a text out of context, or he ends up with a pretext! Every verse on the subject must be considered before a valid conclusion can be reached regarding a doctrine.

First John 2:28 tells the other side of the story: *And now, little children, abide in him; that, when he shall appear, we may have confidence, and not be ashamed before him at his coming.* This verse starts with His appearing and ends with His coming, and says that when He comes, there will be many who are *ashamed.* Now, if they were perfect, they wouldn't be ashamed. So the idea that one must lead a sinless life in order to go in the Rapture does not agree with the rest of the Bible. One is not ashamed if he is perfect. Hence, the imperfect are raptured.

The Bible also reveals that those persons *saved by fire* stand before the Lord (see 1 Corinthians 3:15). They made heaven "by the skin of their teeth," so to speak. The only way any of us can stand in a perfected state before Jesus Christ in that hour is through the merits of His shed blood. Second Corinthians 5:21 declares, *For* [God] *hath made him to be sin for us, who knew no sin; that we might be made the righteousness of God in him.* This is our only perfection. In addition, the Bible states that every believer is a member of the body of Christ (see 1 Corinthians 12:12,13). Should only those

35

who meet a certain standard of spirituality be taken, the body of Jesus Christ would be dismembered and disfigured. This is an impossibility. I am so glad that 1 Corinthians 15:51, 52 states that *we shall ALL be changed, in a moment, in the twinkling of an eye, at the last trump.*

Can anyone know the day and the hour of the Rapture?

No. In Matthew 24:36, Christ himself states that the Rapture is a signless, timeless event. Therefore, we know that it is imminent, meaning that it could happen at any moment.

How can one be prepared for the Rapture?

Since 1 Thessalonians 4:16,17 tells us that when Christ comes, *the dead in Christ shall rise first; then we which are alive and remain shall be caught up together with them in the clouds, to meet the Lord*, it is abundantly clear that the Rapture is only for those who are *in Christ*. In order for a person to be *in Christ,* he must have a personal experience with the Lord Jesus. This takes place when one acts upon John 1:12: *As many as received him, to them gave he power to become the sons of God, even to them that believe on his name.*

Are you absolutely certain that the Rapture is going to happen?

Yes. I've got the Word of my God on it! Jesus is my God, and if He said it, I believe it. In John 14:1-3, He said, *Let not your heart be troubled: ye believe in God, believe also in me. In my Father's house are many mansions: if it were not so, I would have told you. I go to prepare a place for you. And if I go and prepare a place for you, I will come again, and receive you unto myself; that where I am, there ye may be also.* That passage of Scripture has to do with the time when we are transported and transfigured to be like Jesus (see 1 John 3:2)— otherwise known as the Rapture.

Will the Rapture bring both blessing and sorrow?

Yes. Some will be *ashamed* (1 John 2:28) and some will be full of joy. That's why, in 1 Thessalonians 2:19, Paul said, *For what is our hope, or joy, or crown of rejoicing?* What is going to bring me this thrill? This crown! He says, *Are not even ye in the presence of our Lord Jesus Christ at his coming?* (verse 19). He was saying, "I'm going to present you— those I've won to Christ from Rome to Corinth—before the Lord, and that is going to be my joy." But think of the multitudes who will stand before the Lord empty-handed. These are people who have been saved for years, but have no record of service—none whatsoever. They have never won a single soul to Christ.

37

There will be no scales at the Great Judgment Day at the end of the world whereby one is admitted to heaven if his good works outweigh the bad and vice-versa. An individual can be saved only by God's grace (unmerited favor), not through works (Ephesians 2:8,9). Second Timothy 1:9 states: *Who hath saved us, and called us with an holy calling, not according to our works, but according to his own purpose and grace.*

However, there *is* a system of balances found in the Scriptures when it comes to *rewards*. Remember, one is neither saved nor kept by works. He *is*, however, to work because of the salvation he already possesses. Ephesians 2:10 gives clear evidence of this fact: *For we are his workmanship, created in Christ Jesus unto good works.* The Christian's "works" following salvation will be weighed on God's scales and put through His judgment fire. Thus, a system of addition and subtraction *can* be found at the Judgment Seat of Christ.

The Bible also plainly states that a Christian can accumulate rewards while he is on earth, and then *lose* them before his death, or before the Rapture, *by foolish living.* That's right. A Christian cannot live in sin without suffering the consequences—not the loss of his salvation, but of his rewards. Remember 1 Corinthians 3:15, *He shall suffer loss: but he himself shall be saved; yet so as by fire.* Now consider 2 John 8: *Look to yourselves, that we lose not those things which we have wrought, but that we receive a full reward.*

Consider also Revelation 3:11: *Hold that fast which thou hast, that no man take thy crown.* In 1 Corinthians 9:27, Paul says, *But I keep under my body, and bring it into subjection: lest that by any means, when I have preached to others, I myself should be a castaway.* The Greek word for *castaway* means "disapproved" or "put on the shelf." Paul knew that he could lose all his rewards for heroic service if he allowed his flesh to rule his life rather than the Holy Spirit. If this could happen to the man who probably accumulated more "spiritual points" toward rewards than any other man, it can happen to you and me!

Second Corinthians 11:23-26 lists Paul's service record: *In labours more abundant, in stripes above measure, in prisons more frequent, in deaths oft. Of the Jews five times received I forty stripes save one. Thrice was I beaten with rods, once was I stoned, thrice I suffered shipwreck, a night and a day I have been in the deep* [clinging to life in the ocean]; *In journeyings often, in perils of waters, in perils of robbers, in perils by mine own countrymen, in perils by the heathen, in perils in the city, in perils in the wilderness, in perils in the sea, in perils among false brethren.*

Yes, Paul could have lost all of his rewards if he had let his flesh control him instead of the Lord. But he didn't! Hear him again—just before he paid the supreme sacrifice (his life)—in 2 Timothy 4:7: *I have fought a good fight, I have finished my course, I have kept the faith: Henceforth there is laid up for me a crown of righteousness, which the Lord, the righteous judge, shall give me at that day* [the day of Christ's "bema" or Judgment Seat investigation]: *and not to me only, but unto ALL them also that love his appearing.*

What a contrast to some Christians who find it easier to lie in bed rather than go to God's house; easier not to tithe, not to read the Bible, not to pray, not to win souls, not to live in the Spirit—those whose reward will be nothing but ashes. What a contrast also to those who have let the flesh take control at some point in the Christian life. Their rewards, earned through years of service, have been lost because of some foolish unfulfilling habit, a beautiful, flirtatious face, or the desire to travel to heaven via worldly pathways.

I don't know all that will be brought to light at that day, but I do know the first question we are going to be asked: "Did you win souls?" It is also the last thing Jesus asked us to do: *Ye shall be witnesses unto me...And when he had spoken these things, while they beheld, he was taken up; and a cloud received him out of their sight* (Acts 1:8,9).

We will also be asked what we did with our finances. *He which soweth sparingly shall reap also sparingly; and he which soweth bountifully shall reap also bountifully* (2 Corinthians 9:6).

There are so many signs mentioned in the Bible. Do any of these signs point to the Rapture?

Absolutely not. The Rapture is what I call a "signless" event. If you will study Revelation 4:1, which says, *Come up hither,* you will know that chapter 4 refers to believers, because they are laying crowns at Jesus' feet (see verses 10, 11) and you can't get crowns until the time that is called *the resurrection of the just* (Luke 14:14). So the Rapture has already occurred. The "just" now have their crowns, and are laying them at Jesus' feet. All this transpires before the Tribulation period, which begins in Revelation chapter 6 and continues through chapter 18.

So the Rapture happens suddenly, without a sign.

Could the Rapture happen at any moment?

Yes.

There have been so many sightings of UFOs in Belgium and other places around the world, even here in the United States; yet there is still no practical explanation of UFOs. What part—if any—do UFOs play in Bible prophecy?

I love this! A lot of people do not realize that the Bible teaches that *Satan is not in hell!* He is *the prince of the power of the air* [airways] (Ephesians 2:2). That is why we wrestle *against spiritual wickedness* [demon wickedness] *in high places* (Ephesians 6:12). Satan will remain in the heavenlies until Revelation 12:12, when he is cast out to earth. *Woe to the inhabiters of the earth and of the sea! for the devil is come down unto you, having great wrath, because he knoweth that he hath but a short time.*

Right now millions, perhaps billions, of demonic spirits fill the heavenlies. And it's interesting to note that when Elijah was taken up to heaven alive (a picture of the Rapture), *a chariot of fire* (2 Kings 2:11) came to get him, manned undoubtedly by angelic beings. Then Elijah was swept away by a whirlwind into heaven—the exact way a UFO apparently travels.

But my favorite is Ezekiel 1. In verse 4, Ezekiel sees a *whirlwind* [coming] *out of the north*—where God's throne is (see Isaiah 14:12-14). Ezekiel 1:5,6 says it was manned by *four living creatures,* and verse 14 says it traveled like a *flash of lightning*—as do most UFOs.

Recently four UFOs showed up on radar screens in Belgium. For the first time, these UFO sightings were captured on radar. They could drop thousands of feet in a second, which would kill any human being, but not angelic beings. Not only that, Ezekiel 1:16 says *the wheels* [or body] of this chariot was like *beryl*. Beryllium (a derivative of beryl) is what is used in our spacecraft today to withstand the heat and friction of outer-space travel. So it could be that chariots, manned by angels, would come to get us at the Rapture. Ridiculous? Then explain 2 Kings 2:11, which tells how Elijah was caught up by a whirlwind into heaven!

Everyone today is concerned about the economy. Will there be a major economic depression before the Rapture?

This could easily happen, and it could overlap, because during the Tribulation the economy will become horrendous. It will be so bad that the Prophet Ezekiel said, *They shall cast their silver in the streets, and their gold shall be removed* (Ezekiel 7:19). Confiscated! In Revelation 18:10, we see Babylon burning, *For in one hour is thy judgment come.* Verse 11 shows the merchants of the earth weeping. Why? Because in the verses that follow, twenty-eight of their luxurious baubles have been destroyed. Verse 19 says that great riches are made nothing in the space of one hour. That will happen during the seven years of Tribulation.

We might be seeing some recessionary trends right now leading up to that moment, because Jesus is coming soon!

What is the pre-wrath Rapture theory, and how do you feel about it?

That is the new theory presented by Dr. Marvin Rosenthal, former head of Friends of Israel and proponent of the pre-wrath theory, and he's a great man. He says that we go through the seal judgments as a Church (see Revelation 6). Then Revelation 8:1 says, *There was silence in heaven about the space of half an hour.* There is fear in heaven as the wrath of God is about to be poured out, through the seven vial—or bowl—judgments. So Dr. Rosenthal says we will go through the seal judgments but will miss the wrath judgments. Hence, it is called the "pre-wrath Rapture" theory.

However, I don't believe this is how it will happen.

What about post-Tribulationism?

This theory destroys both the doctrine of imminence and teaching of dispensationalism. *Imminence* means "at any moment." The Rapture is not based on any specific set of signs because it is imminent—it could happen at any moment. This is the reason I believe the signs are fulfilled after the Rapture. Remember, the Rapture takes place in Revelation 4:1, and the signs begin in chapter 6. The signs point to the Revelation, or Christ's return to the earth (Revelation 19:11). This event is not based on the Bible teaching of imminence. One can definitely know when it will transpire by the signs pointing to it in Revelation, chapters 6 to 18. When one studies Acts 1:11, Philippians 3:20, Colossians 3:4, 1 Timothy 6:14, James 5:8, and 2 Peter 3:3,4, he notices that these passages mention Christ's coming for His own, without any specific timetable. This is because the Rapture is connected with imminency while the Revelation is not.

As you know, *pre* means "before" and *post* means "after." So those who adhere to the post-Tribulation theory say that the Church will go through the seven years of Tribulation and will meet Christ at the other end, then come right back with Him.

I call this the *Yo-Yo Theory* in my video study, *The Great Escape.* I have a friend who is in the ministry, and we love each other. But he believes the Church will go through the seven years of Tribulation. I believe we won't.

This makes me a *pre-Tribulationist,* while he is a *post-Tribulationist.* Recently, he came to see me and said, "Look at this headline! Jesus is coming soon!" I said, "Amen." He said, "We're going to see Him soon." I said, "Yes, we are. And I'll see Him seven years sooner than you will! So take care of my car while I'm gone!"

Is there a scripture that would support the post-Tribulation Rapture theory?

I believe in order to prove that particular premise, a lot of Scripture would have to be twisted. Again, Scripture does weigh in favor of imminency—that the return of Christ could happen at any moment.

Do you believe the pre-Tribulation Rapture theory?

Yes. I also believe in a literal, dispensational interpretation of God's Word. Without such an interpretation, one can only encounter mass confusion. Second Timothy 2:15 states: *Study to show thyself approved unto God, a workman that needeth not to be ashamed, rightly dividing the word of truth.* This dividing has to do with dispensations and enables one to arrive at accurate conclusions. Although I have already presented many reasons for my rejection of the teaching that the Church will go through the Tribulation, I would like to add two additional thoughts at this point.

First, as mentioned previously, Daniel's seventieth week (Daniel 9:24-27) is divided into three sections—seven weeks, sixty-two weeks, and one final week. Since the Church had nothing to do with the first sixty-nine weeks, why should she be involved in the final, or seventieth, week? Through logical deduction, one sees that, since only Israel was involved in the sixty-nine weeks of the past, only she could be involved in the final, seventieth week, which is the Tribulation hour. I quote Daniel 9:24 in its entirety: *Seventy weeks are determined upon thy people and upon thy holy city, to finish the transgression, and to make an end of sins, and to make reconciliation for iniquity, and to bring in everlasting righteousness, and to seal up the vision and prophecy, and to anoint the most Holy.*

Secondly, Revelation 3:10 states: *Because thou hast kept the word of my patience, I also will keep thee from the hour of temptation, which shall come upon all the world, to try them that dwell upon the earth.* The original wording here is "earth dwellers." We Christians often sing, "This world is not my home; I'm just passing through." This is a true statement because Christians are not earthly, or earth dwellers. Only the unsaved are called by this name. Thus, all those who have been ransomed by the blood of the Lord Jesus Christ are kept out of the hour of Tribulation, which is only for the earthly unsaved or earth dwellers.

Some people believe that Christians will be taken in the middle of the Tribulation. Do you believe that?

No, because that would destroy the doctrine of imminency, which means that Christ can come at any moment. If He comes in the middle of the Tribulation hour, then we know the day and hour if this is the Rapture, because we would have only 1,260 days left (see Revelation 11:3). So that scripture is talking about His Revelation. We will know the day and hour of the Revelation, but we will not know the day or hour of the Rapture. Anything that would happen in the middle of the Tribulation or at some other point will destroy this doctrine of imminency that Christ could come at any moment.

Of whom is the bride of Christ composed?

The bride of Christ is composed of everyone who was saved from the Day of Pentecost onward. This includes everyone who has received Christ until the Rapture *(rapio)* takes place in 1 Thessalonians 4:16. So from Pentecost to the Rapture, we have the bride of Christ.

At what stage in God's prophetical program does the Church, or Bride, now find herself?

According to the Oriental marriage custom followed in the biblical text, we are now in the *betrothal* stage—promised to Jesus Christ. This is why He wants His people to live *holy* lives. By doing so, we (the Church or Bride) can be presented as *a chaste virgin* to the Saviour (or Bridegroom) as expressed in 2 Corinthians 11:2. The hour is approaching when, following the Rapture and the Judgment Seat of Christ, we shall be presented in a faultless state (see Jude 24 and Revelation 19:7,8) to Him *who loved* [us], *and gave himself for* [us] (Galatians 2:20).

I believe we are about to be called into the heavenlies for that great Marriage Supper, because every single sign leading up to this long-prophesied event is already occurring.

And since every sign is already in progress, that great wedding must occur soon. So it won't be long until we hear, *Come up hither!* (Revelation 4:1).

Then Revelation 19:7 says, *Let us be glad and rejoice, and give honour to him: for the marriage of the Lamb is come, and his wife hath made herself ready.*

What is the "Marriage Supper of the Lamb?"

After all Christians have been judged for service, they are presented in one body (or group) *as a chaste virgin to Christ* (2 Corinthians 11:2). Symbolized as a bride, the Church is clothed in fine, white linen (see Revelation 19:7,8). The Lord Jesus himself is the Bridegroom (see Ephesians 5:25-33). The phrase *the marriage of the Lamb is come* (Revelation 19:7) signifies that the Church's union with Christ has been completed. Then Christ returns to the earth with His own (Revelation 19:14) and the Marriage Supper takes place on earth as all the Old Testament saints and the Tribulation martyrs are summoned to this great feast (see Matthew 22:1-14, 25:1-13; Luke 14:16-24).

The Lamb is Jesus. John said, in John 1:29, *Behold the Lamb of God, which taketh away the sin of the world.* This Marriage Supper occurs when His bride (that's us, the Church) has been united to Him. The union takes place in Revelation 19:7,8, in honor of the Lamb (Jesus).

Every bride likes to think about the honeymoon! How long will the honeymoon be for the bride of Christ?

After we are taken up in the Rapture (see Revelation chapter 4), we return with Christ in Revelation 19:14: *And the armies which were in heaven followed him upon white horses.* Jude verse 14 says, *Behold, the Lord cometh with ten thousands of his saints.* And Revelation 20:4 says, *And they lived and reigned with Christ a thousand years.* The only ones coming back with Him happen to be the Bride —to begin the honeymoon.

If the bride of Christ is composed of people who have the Lord Jesus in their hearts, what about the Old Testament saints? Are they part of the Bride?

No. John the Baptist and even Moses were in that transitory period that was governed by the Law—the Old Covenant. In fact, John 1:17 says, *For the law was given by Moses, but grace* [the new dispensation, or covenant] *and truth came by Jesus Christ.* Now, concerning the salvation of John the Baptist—he did not get into heaven at Pentecost. He came before Pentecost. So Jesus called him a "friend of the bridegroom."

John, then, is considered one of the best men of Bible history but not part of the Bride, nor part of the Old Testament saints. Yet all of these Old Testament figures will still have a glorious future.

The Church began to be formed on the Day of Pentecost and will be completed at the Rapture. Hence, the Old Testament saints are not members of the Church. Also, since the Church is evacuated at the Rapture—before the Tribulation begins (see Revelation 4:1)—one can clearly see that the Tribulation saints who are martyred during this horrendous period do not constitute part of the Church. The Church is definitely that group of blood-washed believers beginning at Pentecost and completed at the Rapture. Both the Old Testament and Tribulation saints are raised when Christ returns to earth, in order that they may be guests at the Marriage Supper of the Lamb on earth (see Daniel 12:2; Revelation 4-6).

The Bible speaks about the "Day of the Lord." Is this during the Tribulation period?

Actually, we have to be careful here in defining this one, because the Day of the Lord BEGINS ONE MINUTE AFTER THE RAPTURE! As soon as Christ comes for His bride, the Day of the Lord immediately begins, and it includes the seven-year period of the Tribulation. It also includes the thousand-year millennial period. So the "Day of the Lord" is actually 1,007 years of time.

That is why, after the 1,000 years, *The day of the Lord will come as a thief in the night; in the which the heavens shall pass away with a great noise, and the elements shall melt with fervent heat, the earth also and the works that are therein shall be burned up* (2 Peter 3:10). That's when He makes the new heavens and the new earth of Revelation 21.

So it would be wrong to use the term, "Day of the Lord," referring to the Rapture.

The term "Day of the Lord" has caused some confusion among Christians, hasn't it?

Yes—for the very reason I have just mentioned. They attempt to make the Day of the Lord synonymous with the Rapture. But that is not possible.

Is there a name for the period of time that follows the Rapture?

Yes. It is called "the Tribulation" and is also often referred to as *Daniel's seventieth week* in Daniel 9:26,27. The Tribulation lasts seven years and is undoubtedly the worst bombardment of tragedy the earth will ever experiece. The final forty-two months, or three and one-half year period, is so terrifying that it is called the *great tribulation* (Revelation 7:14).

3

Heaven

When we get to heaven, will we recognize our loved ones who have gone on before us?

Very definitely. Matthew 17:1 says, *And after six days Jesus taketh Peter, James, and John his brother, and bringeth them up into an high mountain apart, and was transfigured before them.* This is literally a scene of what it will be like when Jesus returns. Suddenly Moses and Elijah appeared with Jesus. Peter said, "Let's make three tabernacles, Jesus— one for You, one for Moses, and one for Elijah." Then Jehovah God spoke and said, *This is my beloved Son* (verse 5). He is the *only* One any of us is to worship!

The disciples did not live in the times of Moses or Elijah. In Bible days there were no photographs. So how could they have known that the two men who appeared with Jesus were Moses and Elijah—except by the Spirit of God? The transfiguration scene is a picture of the Rapture, when the Lord calls us home. At that time we shall know even as we are known (see 1 Corinthians 13:12). This knowledge is ours because we shall be like him; for we shall see him as he is (1 John 3:2).

Another good example is found in Luke 16:22-24, where the rich man, Lazarus, and Abraham recognized one another.

We will know our loved ones!

Will our pets go to heaven? Will they be taken in the Rapture?

The Holy Spirit gave this answer to me when one of our precious partners wrote to us, asking this very question. The Lord came upon me in a beautiful way. May I share this letter with you? I will not give the person's name...thus I can quote directly from my reply:

> Your confidential letter arrived, and my heart was deeply moved as I read it. Please don't feel embarrassed about presenting a question as important as the one you did concerning your pet. Rexella and I love our little cat, Fenica, and feel exactly as you do about this little bundle of love. To answer your question, I can only give my opinion and then attempt to answer it scripturally. I believe that everything on earth is a picture, or pattern, of things in heaven. Thus, during the millennial reign of Christ, the earth is filled with tamed and beautiful animals of all descriptions.

Isaiah 11:6 says, *The wolf also shall dwell with the lamb, and the leopard shall lie down with the kid; and the calf and the young lion and the fatling together; and a little child shall lead them.* Wherever God dwells, the beasts of the earth are plentiful. Furthermore, since earth is a pattern of heaven, *the third heaven* (2 Corinthians 12:2,3) must also be filled with these little bundles of love. I don't believe the return of Christ on *a white horse* (Revelation 19:11) is merely rhetoric. Jesus returns riding this animal because there are beasts in heaven.

On the issue of pets and the Rapture, the Bible does not specifically state anything about animals being taken in the Rapture. However, since God promises that He will not withhold any good thing from those who love Him (see Psalm 84:11), I believe a simple request to the Saviour could cause our desire for our pets to be fulfilled instantaneously. For instance, there are those whose beloved pets went the way of all flesh and died. However, God is able to bring them back from dust and ashes as simply as He does humans, when the dead in Christ shall rise.

As I stated earlier, I believe we will have the animals we loved with us in heaven—not because of the Rapture, but because our requests produce God's restoration of our pets, just like when He raises the dead and recreates our loved ones from dust and ashes.

What actually happens in heaven when Christians are called home "in the twinkling of an eye?"

Immediately there is an investigative judgment of the believer's life: *For we must all appear before the judgment seat of Christ; that every one may receive the things done in his body, according to that he hath done, whether it be good or bad* (2 Corinthians 5:10).

According to Romans 14:12, *Every one of us shall give account of himself to God.* This is not the "Great White Throne" judgment of Revelation 20:11-15, commonly called the "Great Judgment Day." In that judgment, the lost are assigned to the lake of fire. Praise God, no person whose sins have been washed away by the blood of Christ need ever stand with that ungodly multitude to be condemned! Why? Because *the blood of Jesus Christ* [God's] *Son cleanseth us from ALL sin* (1 John 1:7). All means ALL, so the true believer has no listing of wickedness as the books of God are opened. *He that believeth on* [Christ] *is not condemned* (John 3:18). The iniquity that *would* have condemned him was obliterated when he trusted in the shed blood of the

Saviour as payment for his sin. Because of his trust, the believer *shall not come into condemnation; but is passed from death unto life* (John 5:24).

Would you love to join the happiest people in the world and triumphantly shout, *There is therefore now no condemnation to them which are in Christ Jesus* (Romans 8:1)? Then ask Christ to come into your heart and save you—the sooner the better!

Earlier we addressed the question of why some Christians don't like to hear about the coming of the Lord. It's because of the investigative judgment that occurs as soon as we get to heaven. In 2 Corinthians 5, the pronouns *we* and *us* are used twenty-six times, always referring to Christians.

Since believers *cannot* be judged at the Great White Throne judgment, it only stands to reason that the investigation mentioned in 2 Corinthians 5:10 and Romans 14:12 (also called the "bema seat" in the Greek New Testament) has to do with the *service* rendered by them following their salvation. Thus, the "Bema," or Judgment Seat of Christ has to do with rewards for the faithful, not condemnation.

Will all Christians go through this investigation when they get to heaven?

Definitely. All the saved are taken in the Rapture. According to 1 Corinthians 15:51,52,

We shall all be changed, in a moment, in the twinkling of an eye, at the last trump: for the trumpet shall sound, and the dead shall be raised incorruptible, and we [the living] *shall be changed.*

The Rapture brings all Christians into the presence of the Lord. Then, as Romans 14:10 states, *We shall all stand before the judgment seat of Christ.* This disproves the teaching that only those who are perfect will be called upward. The Bible plainly states that *we must ALL appear before the judgment seat of Christ; that EVERY ONE may receive the things done in his body...whether it be good or bad* (2 Corinthians 5:10). This certainly does not denote perfection!

Again, in 1 John 2:28, we find, *And now, little children* [believers], *abide in him; that, when he shall appear, we may have confidence, and not be ashamed before him at his coming.* If Christ comes only for the perfect, how is it that multitudes of His children are *ashamed* at this great meeting? Only an *imperfect* individual will be ashamed before Him. Believe the Bible! Every person who has been genuinely "born again" will be present at the Judgment Seat of Christ to answer for his service record.

Romans 14:12 says, *Every one of us shall give account of himself to God.* It's easy to judge others, isn't it? But only you will give an account of yourself to God concerning every aspect of your life.

Is it true that one sin can keep you out of heaven?

No. First John 2:28 says, *And now, little children, abide in him; that, when he shall appear, we may have confidence, and not be ashamed before him at his coming.* Those who are ashamed have done something wrong—but they are still there. They went at the Rapture but did not have an abundant entrance. Scripture indicates there is more than one way to enter. There is the "abundant way" (see 2 Peter 1:11), and there is the way *by fire* (1 Corinthians 3:15), which I would call entrance into heaven by the "skin of one's teeth" method.

If one sin could keep a man out of heaven, no one could get there. Why? Have you ever had a foolish thought? Of course! Proverbs 24:9 says, *The thought of foolishness is sin.* Have you ever had a lack of faith? Of course! *Whatsoever is not of faith is sin* (Romans 14:23). Have you ever felt that God wanted you to do something in His service—and you didn't do it? It's sin! *Therefore to him that knoweth to do good, and doeth it not, to him it is sin* (James 4:17). So there are sins of commission and sins of omission. The sins of commission have to do with outright sin. The sins of omission have to do with not doing what we know we are supposed to do for God.

But thank God for His grace! For *where sin abounded, grace did much more abound* (Romans 5:20). Grace is God's favor. The presence of sin in one's life might mean that person will lose his or her rewards, but not salvation itself. Remember, one does not lose rewards because of his perfection. Rewards are lost because of disobedience, and disobedience is sin (see Romans 5:19). Nevertheless, the disobedient are taken in the Rapture and are present at the Judgment Seat of Christ.

Will it be a time of sorrow for some of God's people when they see the Lord?

Yes. The *ashamed* (1 John 2:28) and those who *suffer loss* (1 Corinthians 3:15) will shed many tears. Revelation 1:19 says, *Write the things which thou hast seen, and the things which are, and the things which shall be hereafter.* If one studies the Book of Revelation chronologically, he finds that it reveals *things which thou hast seen* (chapter 1, *past*), the *things which are* (chapters 2 and 3, *present*), and *the things which shall be* (chapters 4 through 22, *future*).

Now watch this: the seven-year Tribulation occurs in Revelation 6 through 18. Christ comes back as *King of kings* (chapter 19, verse 16), and the 1,000-year reign of Christ occurs (chapter 20, verse 4). Then in

Revelation 21:4, after the seven years of Tribulation, and after the 1,000-year Millennium, *God shall wipe away all tears from their eyes.* This verse does not imply that upon one's entrance into heaven all tears are immediately wiped away. Instead, by studying the passage in its chronological setting, we see that the tears are wiped away *after God's people have been in His presence for 1,000 years!* Those weeping had been raptured and judged for their service. They didn't weep constantly, but spasmodically and intermittently, when they thought about their lack of love and their lack of service for Christ. They wept each time they thought of what they could have done—but didn't do. Then—ten centuries later—God wipes away the tears they shed as a result of their disobedience. Only then do sorrow and crying cease eternally.

Many Christians think they can get away with their selfish way of life. They find it easier to stay in bed on Sunday morning than to assemble themselves with God's people as the Holy Spirit commands in Hebrews 10:25. They find it more pleasurable to watch TV by the hour than to *search the scriptures* (John 5:39). They find it easier to golf, bowl, ski, or become a sports fanatic than to *continue in prayer* (Colossians 4:2). They find it more convenient to use God's money (the tithe and offerings) for cars, home furnishings, clothes, restaurants, and other creature comforts than to support the local church and the proclamation of the gospel to all the world. They certainly find it more convenient to remain speechless concerning Christ than to witness. After all, one could be branded a fool, fanatic, idiot, imbecile, or "Jesus freak" if he talks too much about the Saviour. It is much less complicated to be *conformed to this world* than to be *transformed* for Christ (Romans 12:2). Still, Jesus is coming soon, and many Christians—perhaps even some reading this book—will be totally ashamed as the Lord Jesus makes His full inspection of their lackadaisical, slothful lives.

So there will not only be shame, but times of weeping for 1,007 years. Then God says, "Enough!" At that point there will be no more sorrow. I encourage you to study Revelation 21:4 for a greater understanding here.

4

The Tribulation and the Antichrist

You have said that some people will accept the Lord during the Tribulation. Does the Bible give specific details of how people can survive during this time?

First of all, individuals who do not receive the mark of the beast will be killed. Revelation 20:4 says, *I saw the souls of them that were beheaded for the witness of Jesus, and for the word of God, and which had not worshipped the beast, neither his image, neither had received his mark.* That is the "666" mark. If people want to survive, they will have to take the mark, for without it, they cannot buy or sell. *He causeth all, both small and great, rich and poor, free and bond, to receive a mark in their right hand, or in their foreheads: and that no man might buy or sell, save he that had the mark, or the name of the beast, or the number of his name* (Revelation 13:16,17).

On the other hand, I am certain there will be ways to bypass accepting the mark and still survive. For instance, Jesus, speaking about this particular hour, said to His people, *Then let them which be in Judaea flee into the mountains* (Matthew 24:16). Perhaps they will raise their own crops. Not all will die as believers, for when Christ returns and judges the nations (see Matthew 25:31-46), there are millions upon millions of Christians still alive, even though they rejected the mark. So there has to be a way provided by God to get around accepting the mark of the beast.

Where does the Bible teach that the Tribulation will be the earth's worst time in history?

Jeremiah 30:7 says, *Alas! for that day is great, so that none is like it.* Daniel 12:1 says, *There shall be a time of trouble, such as never was since there was a nation.* Then Jesus said, in Matthew 24:21, *For then shall be great tribulation, such as was not since the beginning of the world to this time, no, nor ever shall be.*

Numerous Bible passages describe this time. Joel 2:2 describes it as *a day of darkness and of gloominess, a day of clouds and of thick darkness...there hath not been ever the like, neither shall be any more after it, even to the years of many generations.* Each prophet and Christ say identically the same thing—there will *never* have been anything like it in past history, nor shall there ever be anything like it in the future!

What actually happens to make the Tribulation such a terrible time?

A total of twenty-one judgments fall upon the earth. They constitute three series of seven judgments each and are described as the seal, trumpet, and vial judgments as follows:

THE SEAL JUDGMENTS

1. The world's greatest dictator (Revelation 6:1,2)
2. The world's greatest war (Revelation 6:3,4)
3. The world's greatest famine (Revelation 6:5,6)
4. The world's greatest death blow (Revelation 6:7,8)
5. The world's greatest persecution (Revelation 6:9,10)
6. The world's greatest ecological disaster (Revelation 6:11,12)
7. The world's greatest hour of fear—actually the lull before the storm! (Revelation 8:1)

THE TRUMPET JUDGMENTS

8. The world's greatest fire (Revelation 8:7)
9. The world's greatest oceanic disturbance (Revelation 8:8,9)
10. The world's greatest pollution of water (Revelation 8:10,11)

11. The world's greatest darkness (Revelation 8:12)
12. The world's greatest pestilential invasion (Revelation 9:1-6)
13. The world's greatest army (Revelation 9:16)
14. The world's greatest storm (Revelation 11:15-19)

THE VIAL JUDGMENTS
15. The world's greatest epidemic (Revelation 16:2)
16. & 17. The world's greatest contamination by blood (Revelation 16:3-7)
18. The world's greatest scorching (Revelation 16:8,9)
19. The world's greatest plague (Revelation 16:10,11)
20. The world's greatest invasion (Revelation 16:12)
21. The world's greatest earthquake (Revelation 16:18)

These twenty-one judgments will unleash unbelievable war, ecological disasters, and atomic catastrophe. *By these three was the third part of men killed, by the fire, and by the smoke, and by the brimstone* (Revelation 9:18). *And blood came out of the winepress, even unto the horse bridles, by the space of a thousand and six hundred furlongs* (Revelation 14:20). According to today's calculations, that is a river of blood 200 miles long—the exact length of the nation of Israel. Think of it! An entire nation saturated and soaked with blood. Thank God, the Rapture is coming! That means we—the church of Jesus Christ—won't be here. The Bride will be at home, at the Marriage, and afterwards return for the Supper.

So the Bible does teach that there will be a nuclear war during the Tribulation?

Definitely! A *third part of men* [was] *killed, by the fire, and by the smoke, and by the brimstone* (Revelation 9:18) (the exact effects of a nuclear blast). Again: A *third part of trees was burnt up, and all green grass was burnt up* (Revelation 8:7). These scriptures clearly reveal a judgment of fire taking place upon earth during the Tribulation. There's more: *A fire goeth before him* (Psalm 97:3). *For, behold, the Lord will come with fire* (Isaiah 66:15). *The flaming flame shall not be quenched* (Ezekiel 20:47). *A fire devoureth before them* (Joel 2:3). Who? The northern army—the Russian army—that moves against Israel. When they are driven back, the prophet says, *I will show wonders in the heavens and in the earth, blood, and fire, and pillars of smoke* (Joel 2:30). *The whole land shall be devoured by the fire of his jealousy* (Zephaniah 1:18). *For, behold, the day cometh, that shall burn as an oven* (Malachi 4:1).

Therefore, both the Old and New Testaments are in agreement concerning a nuclear holocaust.

What terms does the Bible use to describe the Tribulation?
It is called the time of:

1. Punishment (Isaiah 24:20-23)
2. Indignation (Isaiah 26:20,21)
3. Trouble (Jeremiah 30:7)
4. Destruction (Joel 1:15)
5. Darkness (Joel 2:2)
6. Trials (Revelation 3:10)
7. Wrath (Revelation 6:16,17; 1 Thessalonians 1:10, 5:9)
8. Judgment (Revelation 14:7, 19:2)

The Tribulation could not just happen—there must be some kind of an event that would trigger it. What is this event?
This is when the Antichrist arises out of the revived Roman Empire (the European Community, or E.C.) and starts his peace negotiation with the nations. From the night the contract is signed, that is the beginning of the Tribulation hour, the seven-year period of trouble and woe. One can begin the countdown from the moment that peace contract is signed—a total of 2,520 days until Christ's return to earth.

Some people believe the Church—and by that, I mean Christians from all denominations—will go through this terrible, terrible time of Tribulation. Do you believe that?

Absolutely not. My conviction that the Church will NOT go through the Tribulation is based upon the following:

1. The promise to the church in Philadelphia: *Because thou hast kept the word of my patience, I also will keep thee from the hour of temptation, which shall come upon all the world, to try them that dwell upon the earth* (Revelation 3:10). The seven churches of Revelation 2 and 3 represent the professing Church in seven successive epochs from the Day of Pentecost to the time of the Lord's return. Each church fits chronologically into its respective place in the history of Christendom.

The sixth church, called "Philadelphia," escapes the Tribulation hour, but the seventh— "Laodicea"—is rejected by Christ. Its members nauseate the Saviour because of their worldliness and lukewarmness. The *true* believers, *possessing* Christ, are kept from the hour of temptation that immerses our entire planet. Notice that God says, *I also will keep thee from* [not through] *the hour of temptation.*

Now, if He wanted everyone to know that the Church was going to go through the seven-year Tribulation, our God, who wrote this

Book, would have used the Greek word, *dia,* (through) in this passage. Instead, He used the Greek word, *ek,* which means "out of," or "evacuation." It's the same word found in 1 Thessalonians 1:10 which states that Jesus delivers His own *from the wrath to come.* Since the identical Greek word is used in both 1 Thessalonians and Revelation, one can logically deduce that if Christians are exempted from hell, they are also taken out of—or removed from—the midst of the hour that comes upon all the world, the Tribulation. Again, 1 Thessalonians 5:9 states: *For God hath not appointed us to wrath.* AMEN!

2. Another important point regarding this question is the fact that the Church cannot be found in the Book of Revelation after the Rapture call of chapter 4, verse 1, until she returns with Christ following the Tribulation (see Revelation 19:14).

3. The case of the twenty-four elders: In Revelation 4:1, John is told to *Come up hither.* Many believe this pictures the Rapture of the Church prior to the beginning of earth's holocaust. Is this a possibility? Again, my answer is a dogmatic, "Yes!" Why? Because verse 10 states: *The four and twenty elders fall down before him that sat on the throne, and worship him that liveth for ever and ever, and cast their crowns before the throne.* Where did they get those crowns, if one cannot be crowned until *the resurrection of the just* (Luke 14:14)—the Rapture?

Who are these twenty-four elders? The Levitical priesthood was divided into twenty-four groups for service. All Christians are members of the *royal priesthood* (1 Peter 2:9). We conclude, then, that the scene in Revelation 4 and 5, is the direct outcome of the Rapture. The Church is present in heaven as the twenty-four representatives of God's people are singing about the blood of the Lamb (see Revelation 5:9). Notice also that they are arrayed in white garments and have received their crowns before the first seal of judgment is broken in chapter 6. It is an additional blessing to see that they remain in this abode of safety while earth's bombardments are occurring. Once again I emphasize that the Church *cannot be found* in the Book of Revelation during any of the judgments. She is seen returning *with the Saviour* in chapter 19 when the Tribulation is ended.

4. Consider the hinderer—the Holy Spirit: The Christians at Thessalonica were disturbed because they thought the Saviour had returned and they were experiencing the beginning of the "Day of the Lord" or the Tribulation (see 2 Thessalonians 2:1-5). Their fear was intensified by the persecutions they were enduring (see chapter 1, verse 4). Paul wrote to assure them that their fear was unjustified and that, in fact, the "Day of the Lord" *could not have yet* *come* because first there had to be a departure from the faith and, secondly, the lawless one—the super-deceiver—had to be revealed. Paul further stated that the Antichrist could not be made manifest until the One who restrains Antichrist's appearing was removed, namely the Holy Spirit. Paul says, *Only he who now letteth* [hinders] *will let* [hinder], *until he be taken out of the way. And then shall that Wicked* [or wicked one] *be revealed* (2 Thessalonians 2:7,8).

The Holy Spirit lives in the hearts of believers. In fact, our bodies constitute His temple (see 1 Corinthians 6:19). Therefore, when He ceases to hinder the appearing of the Antichrist by removing His restraining influence, His temple—the believers in whom He resides —is removed via the Rapture. I repeat that the lawless one who rules the earth during the Tribulation cannot come to power until the restraining influence of the Holy Spirit, through His temple, is removed. *Receive Christ today. He is coming soon to call us away!*

5. The Tribulation is called "the time of Jacob's trouble": Jacob is Israel (see 2 Kings 17:34). The Tribulation hour is also called "Daniel's seventieth week" (Daniel 9). In history, the first sixty-nine weeks involved Israel (Daniel 9:24). Therefore, why would the seventieth, or final, week not also involve Israel? For what reason would it revert to the church of the Lord Jesus Christ? Simple logistics tell us that Israel experiences the trials of the future. This is why I believe the Tribulation hour is so near. Observing the present Middle East movements and confrontations, one realizes that the greatest war in the annals of history will take place in this area—just as the Bible predicts! The hour is late. Earth's judgment is soon to begin, and Christ may call His children home at any moment. Praise God, the Church will not go through the Tribulation!

If you would like more information about the Rapture, I suggest that you order my video, *The Great Escape,* for an in-depth, one hour and fifteen-minute study on all the reasons why saints will miss the Tribulation period.

There will be some who accept Christ during the Tribulation. Will those Christians survive this Tribulation? When will they get their glorified bodies?

As I stated earlier, the judgment of the nations is recorded in Matthew 25:31-46. And multitudes who were saved during the Tribulation hour (see Revelation 7:14) are allowed to enter into the 1,000-year reign of Christ bodily [with their ordinary bodies]. Now, how did they survive if they could not buy or sell any products without the mark of the beast (see Revelation 13:16,17)? Somehow they found a way to bypass it.

Even in the former Soviet Union, which was under communism for seventy years, there was a way for some Christians to keep the faith. Those who are saved during the Tribulation will get their glorified bodies at the end of the Millennium. The ones who die during the Tribulation hour will get their glorified bodies as Jesus comes back and raises them (see Revelation 20:4,5), and they will enter into the 1,000-year period with their new glorified bodies. But the ones who are alive when He comes back will go into the millennial reign with their old bodies and then get new bodies in Revelation 21:1,2, because that is when He "creates all things new."

How would you describe Daniel's seventieth week?

It will be a period of seven years—eighty-four months, each having 360 days by the old Jewish calendar, for a total of 2,520 days. In Revelation 11:3 and Revelation 12:6, half of this period is recorded as 1,260 days. If you double that, it is 2,520 days. It is a time of unprecedented trouble.

Alas! for that day is great, so that none is like it (Jeremiah 30:7).

This period of time is divided into three sections. The first division comprised seven weeks, or a period of forty-nine years, and had to do with the rebuilding of Jerusalem *in troublous times* (Daniel 9:25). The second division of sixty-two weeks, or 434 years, signaled the time of Christ's death after the rebuilding of Jerusalem. This prophecy was fulfilled exactly on schedule. Christ came and offered himself to Israel, but was rejected and *cut off, but not for himself* (Daniel 9:26). This was the Crucifixion, after the completion of His offer as King. The rebuilding of Jerusalem began on March 14, 445 B.C. and Christ was cut off on schedule. Now Israel must pay the price for rejecting her King. So a final week is coming when the Antichrist will confirm his peace *covenant with many for one week*, or seven years (Daniel 9:27). When the Antichrist usurps the throne that rightfully belongs to Christ, he *shall destroy the city and the sanctuary; and the end thereof shall be with a flood, and unto the end of the war desolations are determined* (Daniel 9:26). This is the time of Jacob's (or Israel's) trouble, resulting from the rejection of Christ. God's chastisement then creates an attitude of acceptance for the true King—the Lord Jesus Christ—at the close of the seventieth week.

There is no doubt about it; Israel travails greatly before the King returns. Jeremiah's prophecy proves it: *For, lo, the days come, saith the Lord, that I will bring again the captivity of my people Israel and Judah, saith the Lord: and I will cause them to return to the land that I gave to their fathers, and they shall possess it. And these are the words that the Lord spake concerning Israel and concerning Judah. For thus saith the Lord; We have heard*

*a voice of trembling, of fear, and not of peace.
Ask ye now, and see whether a man doth travail with child? wherefore do I see every man
with his hands on his loins, as a woman in travail, and all faces are turned into paleness?
Alas! for that day is great, so that none is like
it: it is even the time of Jacob's trouble* (Jeremiah 30:3-7).

Daniel also describes the day of sorrow
when a monstrous anti-Semite dictator, satani-
cally energized, *shall speak great words
against the most High, and shall wear out the
saints of the most High* (Daniel 7:25).

The Lord Jesus himself stated in Matthew
24:9,21,22, *Then shall they deliver you up to
be afflicted, and shall kill you: and ye shall be
hated of all nations for my name's sake...For
then shall be great tribulation, such as was not
since the beginning of the world to this time,
no, nor ever shall be. And except those days
should be shortened, there should no flesh be
saved: but for the elect's* [Israel's] *sake those
days shall be shortened.*

**Since you believe the Book of Revelation is
written chronologically, why do the events
of chapters 12-19 seem to repeat or overlap
those found in chapters 6-8?**

Revelation 1:19 says, *Write the things
which thou hast seen, and the things which
are, and the things which shall be hereafter.*
As previously stated, this is past (chapter 1),

present (chapters 2 and 3), and future (chapters 4 to 22). However, there is a further division which must be studied here in order to make the Book of Revelation perfectly clear. Chapters 4 to 11 picture the seven-year period of Tribulation, and chapter 11 portrays the return of Christ to earth (verses 15-18). Chapters 12-19 depict the identical scene a second time. Thus we find the account of the seven-year period of Tribulation beginning again in chapter 12 and continuing through chapter 19. Christ's return is described in verse 11 of chapter 19. God tells it to us twice to reinforce the significance of its message in our hearts.

There is a verse of Scripture that is often misunderstood: *then shall two be in the field; the one shall be taken, and the other left* **(Matthew 24:40). What does this verse really mean?**

We have to keep every text in context. So we begin at Matthew 24:37-39, *But as the days of Noe were, so shall also the coming of the Son of man be. For as in the days that were before the flood they were eating and drinking, marrying and giving in marriage, until the day that Noe entered into the ark, and knew not until the flood came, and took them all away; so shall also the coming of the Son of man be.*

Now, keeping it all in that context, we look further at Matthew 24:40,41, *Then shall two be in the field; the one shall be taken, and*

77

the other left. Two women shall be grinding at the mill; the one shall be taken, and the other left. That fits the bill. Only two percent of the population of the world knows Jesus Christ as their personal Saviour. Ninety-eight percent do not. Therefore, since we could not have fifty percent of the population being taken out at the Rapture (one taken, one left), this scripture has nothing to do with the Rapture.

But it does tie in with judgment. In Revelation 6:8, *And behold a pale horse: and his name that sat on him was Death, and Hell followed with him. And power was given unto them over the fourth part of the earth, to kill with sword, and with hunger, and with death, and with the beasts of the earth.* I believe this describes the AIDS virus. If one fourth of the world's population of five billion are destroyed in this manner—1,250,000,000 people— that would leave 3,750,000,000.

By the time we get to Revelation 9:18, there is nuclear war. *By these three was the third part of men killed, by the fire, and by the smoke, and by the brimstone.* We now take off another 1,250,000,000, and you have just one half of planet earth left—one out of two, exactly as depicted in Matthew 24:40.

Will Gentiles be saved during the Tribulation?

Yes. Multitudes of Gentiles will be saved during the Tribulation (see Isaiah 2:2,4, 60:3, 62:2; Matthew 13:47-50, 24:13).

How will they be saved?
Through the precious blood of Jesus (see Revelation 7:14).

Will Christians know who the Antichrist is before the Rapture?
Absolutely not. Scripture clearly teaches that the Rapture takes place **before** *that man of sin* makes his appearance, or is *revealed* (2 Thessalonians 2:3,4,8). That's why 2 Thessalonians 2:7 says, *For the mystery of iniquity doth already work: only he who now letteth will let, until he be taken out of the way.*

Since Jesus lives in our hearts (see Romans 8:9), that means we are taken out of the way. Immediately after that, *then shall that Wicked* [Antichrist] *be revealed* (2 Thessalonians 2:8). Only after the hinderer—the Holy Spirit, who lives in the hearts of believers—is removed, will the Church find out who the Antichrist is. Therefore, only those who are left behind will become acquainted with this monstrous dictator at the inception of the Tribulation hour.

Will the Antichrist be an atheistic Jew, or an atheistic Gentile?

I personally believe the Antichrist will be a Gentile, because he comes up out of the revived Roman Empire (see Revelation 13:1), which is the European Community. Therefore, his being a Jew would be very inconsistent with linking him to the European Community. So the Antichrist doesn't have to be a Jew. I think he'll be a Gentile.

You have said that you feel the Antichrist will make a peace contract with Israel. Will he be a man of peace?

I mentioned earlier that the Antichrist will at first come as a man of peace (see Daniel 11:21), but he honors *the God of forces* (verse 38). And though he comes in on the peace platform and makes a contract for seven years with the nations of Israel (see Daniel 9:27), he breaks that contract after three and a half years. *For when they shall say, Peace and safety; then sudden destruction cometh upon them* (1 Thessalonians 5:3). So this man has an ulterior motive to get power, and like a lot of politicians, he changes his mind once he gets it. Watch out!

During World War II, some prophecy teachers said that Benito Mussolini was the Antichrist. Should we ever attempt to name the Antichrist?

No, definitely not! We won't know who the Antichrist is (see 2 Thessalonians 2:7,8), so why should we even get into trying to determine who he is?

People come up with all kinds of formulas to try to determine who the Antichrist is. For instance, some try to determine the number of the Antichrist by taking apart Roman numerals or by applying numbers to letters of the alphabet. They assign "A" as 1, "B" as 2, "C" as 3, and so forth, right on through the alphabet. This can get very involved, as all those characters are changed into numbers and then everything is painstakingly added up. Some even say the Antichrist is the Pope, because the numerals on his crown total "666!" Kissinger's name also adds up to 666 under this theory. Seventh Day Adventists seem to really propagate that idea. However, when you add the characters in the name of their leader, Mary G. White, using the same formula, you also wind up with "666." So don't judge others!

Some even said Mikhail Gorbachev would be the Antichrist, but these people ended up with egg on their faces because he was soon removed from power.

There have always been, and always will be, individuals who claim to know the identity of the Antichrist. They take the number "666"—which is to be the name and mark of the "beast" or Antichrist (see Revelation 13: 15-18)—and then, through all kinds of mathematical formulations, attempt to come to a conclusion. For example, the language of the

Apostle John, who wrote the Book of Revelation, was Aramaic. Thus, one expert concluded that by ascribing numeric values to the Aramaic alphabet, the name "Nero Caesar" (NRON KRS in Aramaic) equaled "666" as follows:

$$
\begin{aligned}
N &= 50 \\
R &= 200 \\
O &= 6 \\
N &= 50 \\
K &= 100 \\
R &= 200 \\
S &= 60 \\
\hline
&\ 666
\end{aligned}
$$

Others have discovered that the numeric values of the Latin alphabet letters spelling out the title of the Pope, "Vicarius Feleii Dei" or "Vicar of Christ," as inscribed on his crown, equal "666."

V = 5	F = 0	D = 500
I = 1	I = 1	E = 0
C = 100	L = 50	I = 1
A = 0	E = 0	
R = 0	I = 1	501
I = 1	I = 1	
V = 5		
S = 0	53	
112		

```
112
 53
501
─────

666
```

Then, again, someone has developed a third alpha-numeric formula using the English alphabet. Beginning with a base of "6" (the number of man in Bible numerology), this number is multiplied by the position of each letter in the alphabet to determine a numeric value for that letter, i.e. A (first letter of the alphabet) x 6 = 6; B (second letter of the alphabet) x 6 = 12; C (third letter of the alphabet) x 6 = 18, and so on, until Z (the 26th letter of the alphabet) x 6 = 156. The complete alphabet and numeric values appear as follows:

A =	6	N =	84
B =	12	O =	90
C =	18	P =	96
D =	24	Q =	102
E =	30	R =	108
F =	36	S =	114
G =	42	T =	120
H =	48	U =	126
I =	54	V =	132
J =	60	W =	138
K =	66	X =	144
L =	72	Y =	150
M =	78	Z =	156

Thus, by adding up the numeric values of the letters composing a name, this person arrives at the following conclusion:

$$
\begin{array}{rl}
K = & 66 \\
I = & 54 \\
S = & 114 \\
S = & 114 \\
I = & 54 \\
N = & 84 \\
G = & 42 \\
E = & 30 \\
R = & 108 \\
\hline
& 666
\end{array}
$$

However, as one can plainly see, there are millions of names which could total "666" using these mathematical systems. Hence, this is all just speculation. The time could be much better spent studying one's Bible, praying, and winning souls! We cannot know who the Antichrist is until he arrives on the scene, and he cannot arrive until the Church is raptured. Instead of looking for Antichrist, Christians should be looking for Jesus— *Looking for that blessed hope, and the glorious appearing of the great God and our Saviour Jesus Christ* (Titus 2:13).

So we can't know the name of the Antichrist. But do you think he's alive right now?

I definitely think he is alive, because of the emergence of the European Community (revived Roman Empire). The Bible teaches that the Antichrist—the final world ruler—will come out of an alignment of ten nations such as the E.C. (see Daniel 2, 7; Revelation 13:1). The E.C. is being formed right now—in our time—for the first time in world history.

Do you believe the Antichrist could make his appearance in the near future?
Yes, because this leader of the ten western nations sits down with Israel at a peace table when Israel signs contracts with many nations (see Daniel 9:27). For 2,500 years, there was no nation called Israel—not until 1948, when she raised up the six-pointed star of David. From 1948 until 1979, Israel was in a constant state of military preparedness for war. Not until 1979 was she willing to make her first concession and actually sign a peace treaty with another nation. Then on Monday, March 26, 1979, Israel and Egypt signed their historic pact.

This contract, however, was neither the sign nor its fulfillment because it lacked basic ingredients. The contract spoken of in Daniel 9:27 must be signed *in the presence of the western leader* (the Antichrist) and with *many nations*. However, the 1979 contract with Egypt was a beginning. I repeat, Israel could not sign peace contracts in 1947 because there was no nation called Israel.

Does the "he" mentioned in Daniel 9 refer to Christ, or the Antichrist?

First of all, let me explain what that means. *He shall confirm the covenant* [of peace] *with many for one week* [seven years, or one "heptad"] (Daniel 9:27). The "he" is not Christ, but Antichrist. Why? Because we must go to the nearest antecedent, and that's *the prince that shall come* (verse 26) that destroys the city, Jerusalem.

Do you believe that the Antichrist will be associated with astrology, witchcraft, and other occult practices?

Yes. Daniel 8:23 says he is a man who understands *dark* [mysterious] *sentences*.

Where does Antichrist get his power? How can he perform all these supernatural feats?

He gets his power directly from Satan, because Revelation 13:4 says that the dragon gave him his power.

Who is the dragon?

Revelation 20:2 says "dragon" is one of the terms for *the Devil...Satan*.

We are told that the first half of the Tribulation will be peaceful, and that during the

second half, violent, horrible things will happen. Why is the first half peaceful?

The leader (Antichrist) who comes out of the revived Roman Empire will portray himself as a man of peace (see Daniel 11:21), but he honors *the God of forces* [armed forces] (Daniel 11:38). He comes to power on a platform of peace. In fact, he gets the nations to sign a peace agreement for seven years. *He shall confirm the covenant* [of peace] *with many for one week* (Daniel 9:27).

In this text, the Hebrew word *heptad* is used for week. One *heptad* is seven years. But in the midst of the *heptad*—after forty-two months, or 1,260 days—this so-called man of peace breaks the contract. He causes the sacrifice and the oblation to cease. So he comes on a peace platform, but he breaks that contract of peace because, actually, he is a man of war.

The Lord Jesus Christ is *The Prince of Peace* (Isaiah 9:6). Satan always tries to counterfeit everything our Lord has done or ever will do. Before Christ returns to earth to set up His kingdom of peace, the super deceiver—called "the Antichrist"—will present himself as the Messiah (or Christ) *and be accepted!* Just as the Lord Jesus came to earth in a body in Bethlehem, He comes again in that body upon His return to earth (the Revelation). However, prior to this glorious event, Satan will enter the body of a man and proclaim himself as God. This is the Antichrist, *who op-*

poseth and exalteth himself above all that is called God, or that is worshipped; so that he as God sitteth in the temple of God, showing himself that he is God (2 Thessalonians 2:4).

The Antichrist, in imitation of Christ, will come into prominence and power by presenting a "peace program" to the nations. The contracts are signed and confirmed in Daniel 9:27. However, in the middle of the seven-year period, the Antichrist dishonors his treaties and makes the last forty-two months the bloodiest in world history. Yes, this master deceiver will actually cause the nations to believe that "world peace" and an "international understanding" among nations have been achieved. Yet, 1 Thessalonians 5:3 tells us that *when they shall say, Peace and safety; then sudden destruction cometh upon them, as travail upon a woman with child; and they shall not escape.* The Antichrist's breaking of his peace covenant leads directly to the events occurring during the second half of the Tribulation.

What are some of the other names given to the Antichrist in the Bible?

The Antichrist is also called the *little horn* (Daniel 7:8, 8:9); *a king of fierce countenance* (Daniel 8:23); *the prince that shall come* (Daniel 9:26); *the* [willful] *king* (Daniel 11:36); *the man of sin...the son of perdition* (2 Thessalonians 2:3); *that Wicked* [one] (2

Thessalonians 2:8); and *the beast* (Revelation 11:7, 13:1-3).

What is the mark of the beast, or Antichrist?

Revelation 13:16-18 says, *He causeth all, both small and great, rich and poor, free and bond, to receive a mark in their right hand, or in their foreheads: And that no man might buy or sell, save he that had the mark, or the name of the beast, or the number of his name. Here is wisdom. Let him that hath understanding count the number of the beast...for it is the number of a man; and his number is Six hundred threescore and six.* We know the interpretation of "600." We also know that a "score" is twenty. Therefore, "three score" equals sixty. Then add six.

So "666" is the number of the beast.

Will it be possible to beat the "666" system?

I have already alluded to that. Unless people accept the mark, they cannot buy or sell (see Revelation 13:17). However, when we study Matthew 25:1-46, we see something wonderful! We see that millions are saved and alive and not put to death, as Revelation 13:15 tells us will happen to those who refuse to worship the beast, his image, and his mark.

How do these millions survive? Only God knows! In Matthew 24:16, those *in Judaea* who are alive during this terrible time are told to *flee into the mountains*. Some will no doubt go to agricultural areas where they will grow their own crops. But there will be millions of survivors who will beat the system somehow. I only saw that recently. And when I did, I said, "Thank You, Lord!"

Who is the false prophet?

The beast—Antichrist—rises out of the E.C. in Revelation 13:1, and he is the infamous end-time political leader so long prophesied. But there is also a false prophet, a world religious leader who rises *out of the earth* (verse 11). He has *two horns like a lamb,* but speaks *as a dragon.* This identifies him with Christianity, because Jesus Christ is the *Lamb of God* (John 1:29). The false prophet will be very deceptive. He is tied in with Christianity but speaks as a dragon. This is a picture of Satan, who is called a dragon in Revelation 20:2. The false prophet is the leader of the one-world church described in Revelation 17.

If the Antichrist is so powerful, what would be the main role of the false prophet? In fact, why would the false prophet even be necessary?

He causes the world to worship the Antichrist. To be specific, he makes an image of the beast and commands that people fall down and worship this image (see Revelation 13:12-15).

How can he do that? Would he perform miracles?

Not only does he perform miracles (see Revelation 13:14), but he actually makes this image of the beast come to life and speak (see Revelation 13:15). We had better not laugh at that, in light of the advancement in technology that gives us talking robots and talking computers! It's already very possible!

How far would this false prophet go in the name of religion? Would he ever execute people if they did not obey him?

Yes. The Bible says that anyone who will not worship the beast will be killed (see Revelation 13:15). And Revelation 20:4 says, *I saw the souls of them that were beheaded* [killed] *for the witness of Jesus, and for the word of God, and which had not worshipped the beast, neither his image, neither had received his mark* [666] *upon their foreheads, or in their hands.*

What eventually happens to the Antichrist and the false prophet?

The Antichrist, called the beast, and the false prophet are *both cast alive into a lake of fire burning with brimstone* (Revelation 19:20). People wonder, "Can that be literal fire? Wouldn't bodies disintegrate?" This is interesting. A thousand years later, Satan is cast into that same place: *And the devil that deceived them was cast into the lake of fire and brimstone, where the beast and the false prophet are* (Revelation 20:10). When the devil is cast into the lake of fire, the beast and the false prophet are still intact—a thousand years later! So they obviously survived the flames, but the smoke of their torment was with them *for ever and ever* (Revelation 14:11).

What is the order of events, as you see them, during the Tribulation?

1. The Tribulation begins with the rise of the Antichrist (out of the E.C.) as the leader of a confederacy of ten western nations (Revelation 13:1).
2. He signs a seven-year peace contract with Israel (Daniel 9:27).
3. After forty-two months, Antichrist breaks the contract (Daniel 9:27).
4. Russia invades Israel from the north (Ezekiel 38:15,16), at a time when Israel is at rest or peace (Ezekiel 38:11). This proves that Russia cannot march against Israel until a world peace contract, or disarmament program, is in effect.
5. Antichrist attempts to destroy God's people, the Jews (Revelation 12).

6. He destroys the world church that helped bring him to power (Revelation 17:16, 17).
7. He proclaims himself as God (2 Thessalonians 2:4-11).
8. He himself is destroyed at Armageddon (Revelation 19) and is cast into the lake of fire (Revelation 19:20).

How will the Tribulation period end?

When Jesus Christ returns with His armies, as King of kings and Lord of lords, the armies of the world are at that time squashed at the battle of Armageddon (see Revelation 19:14-21).

5

Armageddon and the Return of Jesus Christ

What is the Battle of Armageddon?

It is the final suicidal battle against the Lord Jesus Christ by all the world leaders, centered in the Middle East.

The valley of Megiddo is where the Battle of Armageddon will be fought. It is a word-play on the Greek, found in Revelation 16:16. Armageddon will be the most horrendous battle ever.

The armies of the world gather at *Armageddon* (Revelation 16:16), and move from there to the *valley of Jehoshaphat* (Joel 3:2) to await Christ's appearing as He descends from the *mount of Olives* (Zechariah 14:4). Then every soldier that is left from every nation will attack Jerusalem (see Zechariah 14:2). That is where Christ will put down all earth's forces and create a thousand years of Utopian peace on earth.

Can you define the name, "Armageddon"?

Many people associate "Armageddon" with the end of the world. Armageddon does not mean the end of the world. *Armageddon* comes from the Hebrew word meaning "the mount of Megiddo." This is a small mountain located at the end of a broad valley in northern Palestine. So Armageddon describes the *location* where the battle of all battles will be fought on that day when Jesus Christ comes back to earth as *KING OF KINGS, AND LORD OF LORDS* (Revelation 19:16). Verse 14 states that His armies return with Him. And those saints composing His great army will live and reign with Christ for a thousand years ON EARTH (see Revelation 20:4). So the world will go on for *at least* another thousand years after the Battle of Armageddon takes place. Praise the Lord!

To date there has been no battle like the Battle of Armageddon will be. *By these three was the third part of men killed, by the fire, and by the smoke, and by the brimstone* (Revelation 9:18). One third of the earth's population will die! In verses 14,15, God says, *Loose the four angels which are bound in the great river Euphrates...to slay the third part of men.* The Euphrates River runs through Iraq and Syria, so there will be another "Desert Storm!" In fact, that's where it will all begin, as troops converge there to move against Jerusalem.

Where will the Battle of Armageddon be fought?

A lot of people say the Battle of Armageddon will be fought right there in the valley of Megiddo, but I say, "No." That is just the gathering place for the troops of the world before they march into the *valley of Jehoshaphat* (Joel 3:2), located just in front of Jerusalem. I believe this is so because all the armies come to attack Jerusalem (see Zechariah 14:2).

Is Armageddon THE final battle or a series of events?

Actually, it is both. Armageddon is the closing scene of three and one-half years of skirmish in the Middle East. This period begins with Russia's invasion of Israel after the peace contract of Daniel 9:27 is broken in the midst of the Tribulation hour. At that time Rosh, or Russia, moves from the north against Israel (see Ezekiel 38:15,16). Additional participants in this holocaust include the ten kings under the dictatorship of the Antichrist (Daniel 7:24; Revelation 13:1); the kings of the east (Daniel 11:44) under China; and the kings of the south, which would involve much of Africa. So here we have the west (the kings of the ten-nation confederacy), the north (Russia and her European hordes), the east (China and her oriental allies who will cross the Euphrates River to join in the battle), and the south

(Africa and her armies) engaged in the bloodiest battle in the history of the world. Armageddon itself climaxes the campaign as the Lord and His armies appear from heaven. At this point the militarists from the four corners of the earth battle Almighty God and the hosts of heaven (Psalm 2:2; Isaiah 34:2; Zechariah 14:3; Revelation 16:14, 17:14, 19:11,14,15).

Does the Bible describe the Battle of Armageddon?

Yes. Revelation 14:14-20, 16:16-21, and 19:11-21 picture the events occurring at this time. We see that hundreds of millions of men (Revelation 9:16) will engage in this Middle East military confrontation which amounts to earth's greatest power struggle—man and the forces of evil against God. Revelation 19:19-21 telescopes us right into the closing scene of the battle: *And I saw the beast, and the kings of the earth, and their armies, gathered together to make war against him* [the Lord Jesus Christ] *that sat on the horse, and against his army. And the beast was taken, and with him the false prophet that wrought miracles before him, with which he deceived them that had received the mark of the beast, and them that worshipped his image. These both were cast alive into a lake of fire burning with brimstone. And the remnant were slain with the sword of him that sat upon the horse, which sword proceeded out of his mouth: and all the fowls were filled with their flesh.* So great and complete will be the destruction resulting from this battle that the blood of those killed will form a river 200 miles long, rising *even unto the horse bridles* (Revelation 14:20). Seven months will be required to bury the dead (see Ezekiel 39:12).

You are literally saying, then, that all the armies of the world will be gathered in Israel. Why will they be there?

Because of anti-Semitism. The world has always hated the Jew, and my heart bleeds for these people. They have suffered so much under Hitler and all the nations. You see, God loved the Jew in a special way (see Deuteronomy 7:7,8), and He chose them. When He sent His Son, He sent Him to the Jews. *He came unto his own* (John 1:11). When He wanted to give us the law, the commandments, and all the benefits and blessings, He chose the Jews. (Read Romans 9:1-5.)

The devil hates the Jews. Satan has always attempted to eradicate the Jews, because the Jews were responsible for begetting the Saviour, as well as for bringing the Bible into existence. Every book of the Bible was written by a Jew, except for Luke—a Greek who wrote the Book of Luke and the Book of Acts. So sixty-four of the sixty-six books of the Bible were written by Jews.

When Satan is cast out of heaven to earth, his last attempt is to persecute *the woman which brought forth the man child* (Revelation 12:13). That woman is Mary, a Jewess. And by that, we know that this is speaking of Judaism, not Christianity, because this woman in Revelation 12:1 has a crown on her head with twelve stars, symbolizing the twelve tribes of Israel.

Is this hatred for the Jews—fostered by the devil—the reason that all the armies of the world will want to go to war with Israel?

Yes, definitely. It will be Satan's last attempt to obliterate the Jews—but he will not be successful. In fact, he is going to be gloriously defeated.

The Bible speaks of a Rapture, and also of a Revelation. Can you define these two terms?

In Revelation 4:1, we find the Rapture—the "snatching away"—when Jesus says, *Come up hither.* Seven years later, in Revelation 19:11, John says, *And I saw heaven opened, and behold a white horse; and he that sat upon him was called Faithful and True.* In verse 14, Jesus makes His exit from heaven to earth, and the armies in heaven follow. And at that moment, He comes as *King of kings, and Lord of lords* (verse 16).

In Revelation 4:1, He comes as Saviour. In Revelation 19:16, He comes as King. In Revelation 4, He comes *before* the horrendous twenty-one judgments listed in chapters 6 through 18. In chapter 19, He returns with His saints who have missed that terrible, catastrophic time in history.

All of these events are called the Revelation, because in that final book of the Bible, Jesus reveals himself to the entire world. *Behold, he cometh with clouds; and every eye shall see him* (Revelation 1:7). Because He reveals himself as King, we call it His "revealing," or the bigger term, "revelation."

What are the signs that point to the revelation of Christ?

There are so many! A number of these signs, as found in the Old and New Testaments, are:

1. Horseless carriages or automobiles (Nahum 2:3,4)
2. Airplanes (Isaiah 31:5)
3. The desert blossoming as a rose (Isaiah 35:1)
4. The alignment of a ten-nation western confederacy (Daniel 2,7).
5. The knowledge explosion (Daniel 12:4)
6. Great increases in travel (Daniel 12:4)
7. *False Christs, and false prophets* (Matthew 24:5,24; 2 Peter 2:1), *wars and*

rumours of wars (Mark 13:7), famines, earthquakes in divers places, pestilences (Luke 21:11), iniquity abounding (Matthew 24:12), and the *gospel of the kingdom...preached in all the world* (Matthew 24:14)

8. Signs in the sun, moon, and stars (Luke 17:26-30, 21:25-27)
9. The introduction of evil spirits which control cults and false religions (1 Timothy 4:1,2)
10. The nineteen signs of 2 Timothy 3:1-5
11. The hoarding of gold and silver, and its final demise (James 5:1-3)
12. False prophets denying the deity of Christ (2 Peter 2:1-3)
13. Scoffers mocking the second coming of Christ (2 Peter 3:3,4)
14. The invention of the atom bomb (2 Peter 3:10)
15. Lethargy and indifference among God's people (compared to the Laodicean church in Revelation 3:14-16)
16. The judgments described in the Book of Revelation 6-18
    (many of these are identical to the signs found in Matthew 24; Luke 17,21).

These can all happen after we have gone up in the Rapture, but the amazing thing is that *every single one of these prophecies is already in progress!* By that, I mean they are already in the initial stages of fulfillment.

Can anyone know the day and the hour of the "Revelation"—the day when the Lord Jesus will return to earth?

Yes, one can know the exact date Christ will return to the earth. When the Antichrist persuades Israel to sign his international peace contract, one can begin marking days on his calendar. The Battle of Armageddon and Christ's return to the earth will be exactly 2,520 days from the date of this signing. In fact, Dr. John F. Walvoord, President of Dallas Theological Seminary, states: "According to Daniel 9:27, the last seven years leading up to the second coming of Christ will begin with a peace settlement. It will lead to the countdown toward Armageddon and introduce the new world leader who will be destined to become the world dictator, the infamous Antichrist."

I like Dr. Walvoord's statement in his book, *Major Bible Prophecies,* about the night the Antichrist arises out of the revived Roman Empire, which I believe to be the European Community. We are seeing it in the formative stages right now, by the way. The Antichrist makes a seven-year contract (see Daniel 9:27) with Israel and the nations. You can count down from that night exactly 2,520 days (based on the Jewish calendar of 360 days per year) until the return of Jesus Christ to earth.

103

This is not the Rapture—no one knows the day or the hour for that. But you can know the day and hour of the Revelation. That is when Jesus Christ returns with His saints (that's us!). Jude 14 says, *The Lord cometh with ten thousands of his saints.* They had no way of saying "millions" in Bible times, so the Greek term is just "ten thousands times ten thousands."

I repeat—we can know the day when Jesus returns to earth, but we will not know the day of the Rapture, when we meet Him in the clouds.

Are the "Gog" and "Magog" of Revelation 20, the same "Gog" and "Magog" of Ezekiel 38 and 39?

No. Most scholars believe that the terms "Gog" and "Magog" will make such an indelible impression upon the world because of the former Soviet Union's fierceness in the Middle East that, even one thousand years later, the memory will remain vivid. Therefore, the terms "Gog" and "Magog" will be reminders of past brutality—much like the names "Pearl Harbor" and "Hiroshima" are to us today.

Since Armageddon is the closing scene of the Tribulation hour, what comes next?

Following the defeat of the opposing armies, Christ returns and judges the nations (see Matthew 25:31-46) and separates the "sheep" nations from the "goat" nations. The rebels (goats) are purged and go into judgment and punishment (see Matthew 25:41,46). Then those who have been converted (sheep) by accepting the message that the 144,000 Jews preached during the Tribulation hour will go into the millennial, or 1,000-year reign of Christ. It is important to note that those who rejected the message are lost—just as any sinner in any dispensation is lost because he rejected the Saviour. Those who heeded the message—including the Gentile multitudes of Revelation 7:14 and Acts 2:21—are allowed to enter the Millennium.

The sheep are those who have trusted in Christ and have treated the Jews with love. The goat nations are those who have not trusted Christ and have mistreated the Jews. The sheep are allowed to go into the Millennium with human bodies, for they have survived the Tribulation. The goats are cast into hell before the Great Judgment. Matthew 25:46 says, *These shall go away into everlasting punishment,* which indicates a premature judgment for the goats.

Included in the hosts which go into this great millennial hour are the Jews of Old Testament times. They were resurrected at the conclusion of the Tribulation so they, along with the raised Tribulation saints mentioned in Revelation 20:4-6, might be participants in the Millennium on earth (see Daniel 12:2).

Is the return of Christ the beginning of the Millennium, or is there an interval of time there?

There is an interval of forty-five days (see Daniel 12:11,12).

What takes place during this forty-five-day period?

Christ comes and smashes the armies of the world so that there can be perpetual peace for 1,000 years (Revelation 19). Next He gathers together all of His elect Jews from the four winds—literally, the four corners of the earth (Matthew 24:31). Then He separates the sheep and goat nations and judges them (Matthew 25:31-46). The judgment is based on their reception or rejection of Jesus Christ, and their love or hatred for Israel. The goat nations are cast into hell—the lake of fire—at that time (Matthew 25:41-46). Then He binds Satan for that 1,000-year period (Revelation 20:1,2).

Finally He resurrects the Old Testament saints (Daniel 12:2) and the Tribulation saints (Revelation 20:4). Then He judges the fallen angels (see 1 Corinthians 6:3).

What is the first resurrection?

There are seven different resurrections in the Bible. The first six are a part of the "first resurrection" terminology.

These are:

1. When Christ was raised as *the firstfruits* (1 Corinthians 15:23)
2. When *the graves were opened; and many bodies of the saints which slept arose, and came out of the graves...and went into the holy city* (Matthew 27:52)
3. The Rapture when Christ calls His Church home *in the twinkling of an eye* (1 Corinthians 15:52)
4. The resurrection of the two witnesses who are put to death, which I believe to be Moses and Elijah (Revelation 11)
5. The resurrection of the Old Testament saints (Daniel 12:2)
6. The resurrection of the Tribulation saints (Revelation 20:4).

All these constitute the first resurrection.

The second—and final—resurrection is when all are raised for Judgment Day, described in Revelation 20:11-15. The first resurrection is unto life; the final resurrection is unto judgment.

Blessed and holy is he that hath part in the first resurrection: on such the second death hath no power (Revelation 20:6). They shall partake of the tree of life.

6

The Millennium

What is the origin of the word "Millennium?"

That one's easy! *Millennium* comes from two Latin words, *Mille,* meaning "thousand," and *annum,* meaning "year" (after the Latin *biennium*). *Millennium*, then, literally means "one thousand years."

Who lives and reigns with Christ during the thousand-year Millennium?

1. The returning saints (Jude 14; Revelation 19:14)
2. The resurrected Old Testament saints (Daniel 12:2)
3. The resurrected saints of the Tribulation hour (Revelation 20:4)
4. Saints saved during the Tribulation who survived.

What will be the condition of the world during the Millennium?

It will be peaceful—utopian. *They shall beat their swords into plowshares, and their spears into pruninghooks* (Isaiah 2:4). Why? Because the *Prince of Peace* is here (Isaiah 9:6). It will be a time of health, *when the eyes of the blind shall be opened, and the ears of the deaf shall be unstopped. Then shall the lame man leap as an hart, and the tongue of the dumb sing...And an highway shall be there, and a way, and it shall be called The way of holiness; the unclean shall not pass over it; but it shall be for those* [righteous]...*No lion shall be there, nor any ravenous beast shall go up thereon* (Isaiah 35:5,6,8,9).

The earth's motto during this time will be *HOLINESS UNTO THE LORD* (Zechariah 14:20,21). When Christ comes as King of kings and Lord of lords, He also bears the title of "The Holy One," or "Holiness." Universal righteousness will flood the world during this glorious hour!

Everything will be calm, beautiful, and tranquil.

What is "post-millennialism?"

Post means "after," and the teaching of post-millennialism asserts that Christ will come *after* the 1,000-year millennial period is completed. Post-millennialists believe that the world situation will become better and better until perfection is achieved. At that point Christ returns and takes over. This, of course, is nonsense in the light of 2 Timothy 3:13, which states just the opposite: *But evil men and seducers shall wax worse and worse, deceiving, and being deceived.* Then, even after He comes, Revelation 19:15 says Jesus will use a *rod of iron* to put the people under control. If Christ has to do it with a rod of iron, people are not going to be able to do it with their own human efforts. So forget post-millennialism. It is totally wrong! The post-millennial theory is so ridiculous that theologians have practically abandoned the teaching.

What is "amillennialism?"

A means "without." So this teaching states that there is *no millennium!* Its advocates deny Isaiah 11:7 and scores of other Old Testament texts which speak of a time of utopia on earth. The message of Isaiah 35:4,5 is meaningless to these amillennialists who allegorize, symbolize, or figuratize the true teachings of God's Word. Amillennialists believe that Christ comes, destroys the world—and that's the end of everything.

Were amillennialism and post-millennialism doctrines taught by the apostles in the early days?

No. Amillennialism and post-millennialism were not taught by the apostles. First of all, Matthew, then John, Andrew, Peter, Phillip, Thomas, and James—seven in all—taught pre-millennialism. So if you want to be on the

Bible side, the first century apostles taught pre-millennialism.

Then, of course, the Church fathers of the first and second centuries preached pre-millennialism. In the third century, Lactantius and Methodius preached it. It was not until 190 A.D. that Augustine started this stuff, and it has infiltrated our churches ever since.

In order to believe anything other than pre-millennialism, is there a text people would have to ignore?

Yes. Those who believe contrary to pre-millennialism don't ever like to deal with Revelation 20:4. It states, *They lived and reigned with Christ a thousand years.* You've got to do something with that! So we symbolize, spiritualize, and figuratize. Nonsense!

What part does the Millennium play in Bible prophecy?

It is the final day. *One day is with the Lord as a thousand years, and a thousand years as one day* (2 Peter 3:8). God created the world in six days (Genesis 1:31) and *he rested on the seventh day* (Genesis 2:2). Since a day is as a thousand years and a thousand years are as a day, we have six days of labor signifying six thousand years of burdensome toil for humanity—followed by a final seventh day of rest, or *the millennial reign of Christ!*

Revelation 20:4 declares, *they* [the returning, resurrected, and raised saints] *lived and reigned with Christ a thousand years.* Our present calendar indicates that this prophecy is nearly ready to be fulfilled.

From Adam until the birth of Jesus Christ, approximately four thousand years transpired —or figuratively, "four days." Then, from the birth of Christ until the 1990s, almost two more "days" passed. We are less than ten years short of the final two "days" for the total of six thousand years, or the six "days" proposed by Peter. There's a little discrepancy in timetables because of the difference between the Alexandrian and Julian calendars. Nevertheless, we are somewhere around 5,990, with a little less than ten years left. Isn't it thrilling to know that we are almost at the completion of that six day period, and about to enter the millennial age? It will be a day of joy!

What Bible terms are synonymous with the Millennium?

1. *The kingdom of heaven* (Matthew 5:10)
2. *The regeneration* (Matthew 19:28)
3. *The last day* (John 6:40)
4. *The times of refreshing* (Acts 3:19)
5. The *restitution of all things* (Acts 3:21)
6. *The day of Christ* (1 Corinthians 1:8; 2 Corinthians 1:14; Philippians 2:16)
7. *The world to come* (Hebrews 2:5)

113

What conditions characterize the Millennium?

1. PEACE—because Christ, *The Prince of Peace*, reigns (Isaiah 9:6). Isaiah 2:4 speaks of the time when all mankind will *beat their swords into plowshares, and their spears into pruninghooks.* Oh, what a day of rejoicing that will be! Other texts for study are found abundantly in Isaiah: 11:6-9, 32:7,18, 33:5,6, 54:13, 55:12, 60:18, 65:25, 66:12. See also: Ezekiel 28:26, 34:25,28; Micah 4:2,3; Zechariah 19:10.
2. JOY—Isaiah 9:3; Jeremiah 30:18,19; Zephaniah 3:14-17.
3. HOLINESS—Isaiah 1:26,27, 31:6,7, 52:1, 60:21, 60:1-10; Jeremiah 31:23; Ezekiel 36:24-31; Joel 3:21; Zephaniah 3:11,13; Zechariah 8:3.
4. KNOWLEDGE—Isaiah 11:1,2,9; Habakkuk 2:14.
5. HEALTH—Isaiah 33:24; 35:5.

With so many scriptures referring to the Millennium, how can some still say that the entire teaching on the Millennium is built on one chapter of the Bible—Revelation 20—which mentions the thousand years?

The doctrine of the Millennium is *not* built upon a single chapter or verse! It is built upon the scores of texts. I won't go into detail here, but I suggest that you order my video series,

Revelation Revealed, Verse by Verse. In it, I take sixty different texts from the Old Testament to prove that the Bible teaches about the Millennium in not one isolated text, but throughout the Word of God.

When Christ comes in the "revelation" and the Millennium begins, He has a glorified body. We return with Him, so we will also have glorified bodies. Are the people who are taken alive from earth into the Millennium going to have glorified bodies, too?

No. When this division takes place on earth, described in Matthew 25:31-46 as the sheep and the goats being separated, the sheep will go into the Millennium with their mortal bodies. All the rest will have glorified bodies.

This means that the saints who return with Jesus (Revelation 19:14; Jude 14) will have their new glorified bodies. Those who survived the Tribulation hour and who have not been condemned in the judgment of the nations (see Matthew 25:31-46) are allowed to enter the Millennium in their mortal bodies. Since they are in mortal bodies and are able to procreate, many babies will be born during the thousand-year period. They, of course, will also have mortal bodies. Therefore, there will be persons with mortal bodies and persons with spiritual bodies on earth during the Millennium.

Where will the world headquarters of the Millennium be located?

In Jerusalem. This is where the Lord touches down at His second coming to earth (Zechariah 14:4) and where He makes His headquarters (Micah 4:1). Isaiah 2:3 states: *For out of Zion shall go forth the law, and the word of the Lord from Jerusalem.* When Christ comes, the gates of Jerusalem will open to welcome the coming King (see Psalm 24). Psalm 72 describes His reign; Psalm 96 indicates that His coming will be to judge the earth; and Psalm 110:1 predicts that, at the coming of Christ, His enemies will be made His footstool. During the Millennium, multitudes will come from the uttermost parts of the earth to visit the holy city (Isaiah 2:2,3).

What will Christians do during the Millennium?

We will be hovering over the Holy Land in the New Jerusalem (Revelation 21,22), and we will be able to travel like thought itself. We will think something—and we'll be instantly there! We will traverse back and forth from the Holy City to earth. When Jesus was on earth, He could go right through a door if He wanted to. And we will be able to do the same, because *we shall be like him* (1 John 3:2). We will be able to do what He is able to do. We will have the knowledge that He has.

116

We shall know as we are known (see 1 Corinthians 13:12). It's going to be a great day!

Where is the Temple when the millennial sacrifices are offered?

It will be an entirely different temple from the one in which the Antichrist sat during the Tribulation. That one was used from the Rapture until Armageddon. The millennial temple is used for the entire 1,000-year period (Ezekiel 40-48). Notice carefully that this temple comes into existence shortly after Russia's invasion of Israel in Ezekiel 38 and 39. Wow! We are certainly living in the last days!

After the Millennium, what's next?

After the Millennium, we find the disintegration of the world through fire (see 2 Peter 3:10). Revelation 21:1 says, *I saw a new heaven and a new earth.*

In studying Matthew 25, we see that after the Millennium, Satan somehow manages to lead a rebellion on earth. How can that be, after 1,000 years of having Christ with us here on earth?

Remember that Christ has to rule with a *rod of iron* during the Millennium to keep everyone under control. Also remember that there are some who enter into the Millennium in their mortal bodies (see Matthew 25). They still can—and do—produce children during the Millennium, but because Satan is bound (Revelation 20:1,2), there is no enticement to sin among these mortals, their children, grandchildren, and great-grandchildren. However, the children born during the Millennium still possess the old Adamic, or sin-prone, nature. Because Christ rules with a rod of iron, they are kept under control for that thousand-year period. When Satan is again unleashed on earth, these are the ones who are deceived into joining his rebellion. This shows the innate wickedness of the human heart.

Exactly what happens during this rebellion?

After 1,000 years of being bound, Satan is loosed again for a brief season (see Revelation 20:7), because God has always wanted everyone to follow Him by his or her own free will.

So these millennial children are tested, and I'm sad to say that multitudes—after being with Jesus and seeing His sweetness, His tenderness, His love and His compassion—will say, "I want to go with Satan."

It is really the same as at His first coming, when the people were with Jesus and yet refused Him.

Satan organizes and leads this insurrection for a brief period of time. Then fire comes down from God and devours Satan and his followers (see Revelation 20:9). Following this, God's Word states that *the devil that deceived*

them was cast into the lake of fire and brim-
stone, where the beast and the false prophet
are, and shall be tormented day and night for
ever and ever (verse 10).

Will people die during the Millennium?

Yes. There will be death during the thousand-year reign of Christ because the sin nature
will still reside in believers who survived the
Tribulation even though Satan is bound for that
thousand-year period (see Revelation 20:1,2).

There will be death at the end of the millennial reign of Christ, because multitudes, like
the *sand of the sea* (Revelation 20:8), will turn
to Christ. The Lord allows this so mankind can
exercise free will, because God wants a people
who love Him out of choice, not out of force.
He desires that they choose Him out of their
hearts, and decide with their wills that they
want Him.

So humans will die during the Millennium
because *the wages of sin is death* (Romans
6:23). *Sin, when it is finished, bringeth forth
death* (James 1:15).

7

The Judgment Seat of Christ

Does the Bible talk about the Judgment Seat and what is going to happen there?

Yes. The Judgment Seat of Christ is clearly portrayed in 1 Corinthians 3:11-15: *For other foundation can no man lay than that is laid, which is Jesus Christ. Now if any man build upon this foundation gold, silver, precious stones, wood, hay, stubble; Every man's work shall be made manifest: for the day shall declare it, because it shall be revealed by fire; and the fire shall try every man's work of what sort it is. If any man's work abide which he hath built thereupon, he shall receive a reward. If any man's work shall be burned, he shall suffer loss: but he himself shall be saved; yet so as by fire.*

One cannot lose his salvation—only his rewards. Notice verse 15: *If any man's work shall be burned, he shall suffer loss: but he himself shall be saved; yet so as by fire.* Here is a text which incorporates the terms "lost" and "saved" in one breath. *Watch it—this is extremely important:* because the believer's work of service upon earth has been bad, or improperly motivated, the fire of God reduces this service of wood, hay, and stubble to an incinerated pile of ashes. All of his life's service is lost! All of his rewards are also lost because one does not obtain heaven's "Oscar" or "Emmy" for a pile of ashes. However, even though the believer suffers loss, he himself remains saved—by fire, or by the skin of his teeth!

First Corinthians 3:11-15 is speaking to believers, because they are the ones who are building on the foundation of Jesus Christ—and only believers can do that. But they are building with two different types of materials. You see, it isn't enough to just work for the Lord. If you have the wrong motive, there will be no rewards. And He is going to judge motives. *Therefore judge nothing before the time, until the Lord come, who both will bring to light the hidden things of darkness, and will make manifest the counsels* [motives] *of the hearts: and then shall every man have praise of God* (1 Corinthians 4:5).

Service and works done with the pure motive of glorifying Jesus Christ will be rewarded with gold, silver, and precious stones. Service and works done for self-adulation, praise, or public adoration will be burned up as wood, hay, and stubble. God takes these two kinds of works and puts them in the fires of testing.

Gold, silver, and precious stones come out better—purified. Wood, hay, and stubble are reduced to nothing but an incinerated pile of ashes.

What shall it be for you, Christian? The Bible says that those having gold, silver, and precious stones will receive a reward. There will be crowns to be laid at the feet of Jesus (see Revelation 4:10,11). If works and service are not performed out of the right motive, the Bible says there will be nothing but a pile of ashes to lay at the feet of Jesus. "Here, Jesus, my service wasn't what it should have been. I did it for *me,* not You." That realization will make the poor believer *ashamed* (see 1 John 2:28).

If you sing in the choir, why do you sing? If you send in your tithe every week, why do you tithe?

Our motives must be pure!

What is the meaning of that portion of 1 Corinthians 3:12, which has to do with gold, silver, and precious stones?

The Bible also teaches that multitudes of believers will appear before Christ with *confidence* (see 1 John 2:28). The confident will see their works of gold, silver, and precious stones untouched by the fire of God. Genuine service for the Saviour will not result in piles of ashes. Heaven's "Oscars" and "Emmys" are presented to those who build upon (1) the foundation of Christ (see 1 Corinthians 3:11), and (2) the glory of Christ: *And whatsoever ye do in word or deed, do all in the name of the Lord Jesus, giving thanks to God and the Father by him* (Colossians 3:17).

Some Christians serve God for self-glory, knowing that they will receive praise and recognition for the service they render. Not only are the believer's works investigated at the Judgment Seat of Christ, but the *motives* behind the works as well! First Corinthians 4:5 tells us, *The Lord...will make manifest the counsels of the hearts.* Those who seek fame, fortune, honor, prestige, and glory will exchange gold, silver, and precious stones for ashes. What a sad ending for a lifetime of Christian service! My question to all believers is, *"Will YOUR present service stand the test of God's fiery inspection?"*

8

The Great White Throne
Judgment

After this season of rebellion on earth during the period following the Millennium, the Bible says Satan is cast into the lake of fire. What happens next?

The Great White Throne Judgment occurs for all sinners. Satan has just been cast into the lake of fire (Revelation 20:10). Verses 11-15 say, *I saw a great white throne, and him that sat on it* [Jesus], *from whose face the earth and the heaven fled away; and there was found no place for them. And I saw the dead, small and great, stand before God; and the books were opened: and another book was opened, which is the book of life: and the dead were judged out of those things which were written in the books, according to their works. And the sea gave up the dead which were in it; and death and hell delivered up the dead which were in them: and they were judged every man according to their works. And death and hell were cast into the lake of fire. This is the sec-*

ond death (the final penitentiary). *And whosoever was not found written in the book of life was cast into the lake of fire.*

God is no respecter of persons (see Romans 2:11). If we don't come to Christ and ask to be forgiven of our sins, we'll stand there with the small and great and answer for it.

Will all the wicked be resurrected for this judgment?

Yes, definitely. This fact is clearly stated in John 5:28,29: *For the hour is coming, in the which all that are in the graves shall hear his voice, and shall come forth; they that have done good, unto the resurrection of life; and they that have done evil, unto the resurrection of damnation.* So again, there are two resurrections—life and damnation. *There shall be a resurrection of the dead, both of the just and unjust* (Acts 24:15).

Who will be turned away from heaven at this judgment?

Revelation 21:8 and 22:15 describe those who are not allowed to enter heaven as follows: *But the fearful, and unbelieving, and the abominable, and murderers, and whoremongers, and sorcerers, and idolaters, and all liars, shall have their part in the lake which burneth with fire and brimstone: which is the second death...For without* [outside of heaven] *are dogs, and sorcerers, and whoremongers, and murderers, and idolaters, and whosoever loveth and maketh a lie.* This description, combined with additional sins found in Romans 1:24-32 and 1 Corinthians 6:9,10, provides a comprehensive picture of those who are damned for all eternity:

1. *The fearful*—those who do not accept Christ to escape being ridiculed (Matthew 10:32).
2. *Unbelievers*—those who do not believe and receive the Lord Jesus Christ (John 8:24).
3. *The abominable*—those who engage in wicked practices (Titus 1:11).
4. *Murderers.*
5. *Whoremongers*—those who engage in fornication or consort with prostitutes (Ephesians 5:5-8).
6. *Sorcerers*—those who practice witchcraft, demonism, and follow after the occult. This word comes from the Greek root word, *pharmakeia,* and means "enchantment with drugs." Thus, drug users, addicts, and even pushers (the Greek *pharmakeus*) are included.
7. *Idolaters*—those who worship or reverence anyone or anything other than the living and true God.
8. *Liars* (John 8:44).
9. *Dogs*—false professors (2 Peter 2:22).

10. *Homosexuals* (Romans 1:18-28).
11. *The unrighteous*—those who trust in self, works, a false religious system, or mere "religion" for salvation (Titus 3:5).
12. *Fornicators*—those who engage in premarital and extramarital sex (1 Corinthians 6:9).
13. *The wicked*—those who disregard all morality and moral standards.
14. *The covetous*—those who wish all things for themselves, especially that which belongs to others (Ephesians 5:5-8).
15. *The malicious*—those who willfully seek to destroy the person and property of others (James 1:26).
16. *The envious*—those resentful of others.
17. *Debaters*—those who would rather argue with God than accept His truth.
18. *Deceivers*—those who purposely mislead or betray others (2 Timothy 3:13).
19. *Maligners*—those who speak evil of, defame, or slander others (James 3:2,3).
20. *Whisperers*—gossips!
21. *Backbiters*—those who constantly find fault with others and speak maliciously about them.
22. *Haters of God.*
23. *Despisers*—those filled with contempt toward God and man.
24. *The proud*—those possessing an excessively high opinion of themselves.

25. *Boasters*—those who exalt self.
26. *Inventors of evil things.*
27. *The disobedient to parents.*
28. *Those without understanding* (resulting from unconcern or rejection of the truth).
29. *Covenant breakers*—those who do not keep their word. (The Antichrist is the supreme example of this type of person.)
30. *Those whose affections are contrary to the laws of God and nature.*
31. *The implacable*—those exhibiting extreme stubbornness to the point of refusing to yield to the convicting power of the Holy Spirit (Proverbs 1:24-28; Acts 7:51,52).
32. *The unmerciful*—those who lack compassion (Ephesians 4:32).
33. *Adulterers*—those who practice extramarital sex.
34. *The effeminate*—those generally younger persons in the process of becoming hardened homosexuals or "sodomites."
35. *Abusers of themselves with mankind*—hardened homosexuals (Genesis 19:5).
36. *Thieves.*
37. *Drunkards*—those given to and overcome by alcohol (Proverbs 20:1, 23:20,21; Luke 21:34; Romans 13:13; 1 Corinthians 6:10; Galatians 5:19-21; Ephesians 5:18).

38. *Revilers*—those who use abusive or contemptuous language.
39. *Extortioners*—those who exact money from, or take advantage of, others through violence, threats, or misuse of authority.

Persons who have practiced these sins then—and who are still contaminated by the guilt of them because they have not come to Christ—will be the ones who stand before the Great White Throne as *the books* [are] *opened: and another book* [is] *opened, which is the book of life: and the dead* [are] *judged out of those things which* [are] *written in the books, according to their works* (Revelation 20:12).

I would like to point out one additional verse of Scripture—1 Corinthians 6:11—which states: *And such WERE some of you: but ye are washed, but ye are sanctified, but ye are justified in the name of the Lord Jesus, and by the Spirit of our God.* Oh, the transforming power of the blood of Christ which *cleanseth us from all sin* (1 John 1:7)! Every man is a sinner, guilty before God (see Romans 3:23). Yet God has given every man (see Titus 2:11) a blessed way of escaping the condemnation due him: *He that believeth on* [Christ] *is not condemned: but he that believeth not is condemned already, because he hath not believed in the name of the only begotten Son of God*

(John 3:18). Have *YOU* believed? *WILL* you believe—right now?

Who will be the judge at the Great White Throne Judgment?

The Lord Jesus Christ (see Romans 2:16; John 5:27; Acts 17:31).

In Revelation 20:11, John says, *I saw a great white throne, and him that sat on it.* Who is that? John 5:22 says, *The Father judgeth no man, but hath committed all judgment unto the Son.* Acts 17:31 says, *Because he hath appointed a day, in the which he will judge the world in righteousness by that man whom he hath ordained; whereof he hath given assurance unto all men, in that he hath raised him* [the judge] *from the dead* (Acts 17:31).

The resurrected one is Jesus. Jesus will be the Judge, and He will judge justly.

We have all heard the term "God is keeping the books!" Is this really true? Does God really have a record of each one of us?

Without any shadow of a doubt! God knows all things about us (see Psalm 139:1-4). He even knows our thought life (see Ezekiel 11:5).

I began this book by saying that God is omniscient, meaning that He knows everything about everything, and all things about all things. So He can keep good books! And I am overwhelmed with what the Bible has to say about every one of us.

In Psalm 139:1-4,6, the psalmist speaks about himself in amazement: *O Lord, thou hast searched me, and known me. Thou knowest my downsitting and mine uprising, thou understandest my thought afar off. Thou compassest my path and my lying down, and art acquainted with all my ways. For there is not a word in my tongue, but, lo, O Lord, thou knowest it altogether...Such knowledge is too wonderful for me.*

This is the magnificent, all-knowing God who keeps our records!

Is it true that the present earth and heavens are destroyed after the Great White Throne judgment?

Yes. Second Peter 3:10,11 undoubtedly pictures an explosion similar to a nuclear blast, which completely annihilates the present earth and heavens. Verse 10 states: *The heavens shall pass away with a great noise, and the elements shall melt with fervent heat, the earth also and the works that are therein shall be burned up.* In Matthew 24:35, Jesus himself said, *Heaven and earth shall pass away.* However, this transpires after His millennial reign and the Great Judgment Day have occurred.

What is the purpose of this destruction?

To refine this old world (Isaiah 48:10).

What happens following the destruction of the old earth and heavens?

God creates a new heaven and a new earth: *For, behold, I create new heavens and a new earth: and the former shall not be remembered, nor come into mind* (Isaiah 65:17).

And I saw a new heaven and a new earth: for the first heaven and the first earth were passed away; and there was no more sea. And I John saw the holy city, new Jerusalem, coming down from God out of heaven, prepared as a bride adorned for her husband (Revelation 21:1,2).

And he carried me away in the spirit to a great and high mountain, and showed me that great city, the holy Jerusalem, descending out of heaven from God (Revelation 21:10).

Even so, come, Lord Jesus (Revelation 22:20).

9

Will You Receive Christ?

We really don't have to die, do we?

No. There is a better way. When we come to Jesus, we instantly receive eternal life! I love Titus 1:2, which says, *In hope* [that's the old English word for "guarantee"] *of eternal life, which God, that cannot lie, promised before the world began.* Jesus said, *I am the resurrection, and the life: he that believeth in me, though he were dead, yet shall he live: And whosoever liveth and believeth in me shall never die* (John 11:25,26).

Never die! That means that once you are born again, you can't die. All you do is transfer! *To be absent from the body, and to be present with the Lord* (2 Corinthians 5:8). That's why Paul says, in Philippians 1:21, that *to die is gain.* You close your eyes here—and open them over there! That's eternal life!

Will you receive salvation and make Jesus Christ your Lord?

Here is God's plan of salvation:

● You must admit you are a sinner. *All have sinned* (Romans 3:23). If you choose to remain in your sin, *the wages of sin is death* (Romans 6:23). That means separation from God, eternally.

● But Romans 8:32 says God *spared not his own Son, but delivered him up for us all.* And in 1 Peter 2:24, Christ *bare our sins in his own body on the tree.* That means your sin, my sin, every sin was born away by Him. And as that blood was flowing on Calvary, it was to cleanse you and me, and all who would receive that cleansing from sin. *And the blood of Jesus Christ his Son cleanseth us from all sin* (1 John 1:7). No matter what I've done, no matter what you've done, Jesus paid the price to cleanse us from all sin. *Christ died for the ungodly* (Romans 5:6). "Ungodly" means *all of us!*

● *Whosoever shall call upon the name of the Lord shall be saved* (Romans 10:13). *But as many as received him, to them gave he power to become the sons of God* (John 1:12). Do you see? When you choose Him (receive Him) you become a son. You have had a new birth, a spiritual birth, for you cannot be a son or daughter without a birth. When you receive Christ, you are born again, as explained in John 3.

Will you pray with me?

Pray with me, from your heart, and God will save you right now:

Lord, I know Your coming is near. These prophecies have convinced me that I must prepare for Your coming. I have sinned. But You died for sinners, for the ungodly, for all mankind, and for me. Your blood washes whiter than snow. I trust in the merits of Your shed blood at Calvary to wash me clean at this very moment. Lord Jesus, I receive You. Come into my heart. I pray this in Your holy name, Lord Jesus. Amen.

If you are a backslidden Christian, will you pray with me?

Father, I am convinced that the coming of Your Son is at the door. Like the prodigal son, I have drifted far from You. When the prodigal son returned, his father met him with open arms, and put a ring on his finger and shoes on his feet, because he loved him. As your wayward child, I am returning. Open Your arms for me like the father of the prodigal son did. Forgive my sin. Cleanse me. Give me a new beginning, that I may spend eternity with You, in Jesus' name. Amen.

If you have made a decision for Christ, will you write to us?

If you made either of these decisions—to accept the Lord into your life as a new believer, or to return to Him if you had drifted away—please write to us. We would like to know!

When you write, Rexella and I would like to send you (absolutely free) a little booklet entitled *First Steps in a New Direction.* I think it will help you grow in the Lord.

May God richly bless you as you live for Him until His soon return!

Other Books by Jack Van Impe

AIDS Is for ~~Life~~ Death
Documented factual information about this deadly modern-day plague. Hundreds of authoritative medical and news reports listed alphabetically by subject for instant reference.

11:59...and Counting!
What does the future hold for you and your loved ones? The questions that plague humanity are answered in this detailed account of mankind's march toward the Tribulation, Armageddon, and the hour of Christ's return.

Israel's Final Holocaust
Over 240,000 in print! One of the most helpful explanations of Israel's role in end-time Bible prophecies ever published. What will the final holocaust be...and how will it affect you?

Revelation Revealed
Revised edition! Yes, you *can* understand what many consider to be the most complex book in the Bible. Dr. Van Impe's verse-by-verse teaching reveals the meaning of this prophetic treasure.

Sabotaging the World Church
Exposes the lovelessness among the brethren, using major excerpts from Dr. Van Impe's previous book, *Heart Disease in Christ's Body.* The answer to the problem is found in the Word of God and requires every member of Christ's body to endeavor *to keep the unity of the Spirit in the bond of peace* (Ephesians 4:3).

Sin's Explosion
Though sin permeates and inundates the land, God specializes in bringing sinners to himself when sin is rampant. Includes scores of stirring quotes from great revival leaders. This book is a must for every library.

Unmasking and Triumphing Over
The Spirit of Antichrist
A handbook to enlighten and prepare soldiers of the cross for the battle of the "latter days." Every page is loaded with spiritual armaments for the believer's warfare against satanic powers and beings. A Spirit-empowered volume that will help insure total victory!

The Walking Bible
The "inside" story of Dr. Jack Van Impe. Forty years of the triumphs and tragedies of a remarkable man of God. New updated version includes new chapters and photographs.

YOUR FUTURE—An A-Z Index to Prophecy
An A-Z listing of biblical terms and major prophetic teachings in the Bible. *Your Future* is an exhaustive, easy-to-use reference tool. For the first time you can have fingertip access to finding and understanding all the prophetic scriptures that affect... Your Future!

ALCOHOL: The Beloved Enemy
Liquor and the Bible. Filled with wisdom and reasoning, this important book thoroughly covers the alcohol question. Includes historic background, current research, and statistics that may shock

you. Bible help for a major problem. Every verse on the subject of wine from Genesis to Revelation is explained.

The Baptism of the Holy Spirit
Dr. Van Impe's easy-to-understand study of who the Holy Spirit is, what He does, and why His baptism is for every believer. Includes what the Bible says about the personality, attributes, gifts, fruit, and power of the Holy Spirit.

The Cost of Discipleship and Revival
To be a true follower of Jesus Christ, the Bible says you must take up your cross and die to self. But just what kind of price do you have to pay? Find the answer, plus keys to revival, in the pages of this enlightening book.

Escape the Second Death
Five powerful salvation messages especially directed to the unsaved. A great witnessing tool. Explains the Bible way to be born again.

Exorcism and the Spirit World
What every Christian should know about Satan, demons, and demonic activity. Reveals the dangers of association with the occult, describes Satan worship, and tells how to defeat demon forces through the delivering power of the Holy Spirit.

God! I'm Suffering,
Are You Listening?
Why do good people go through seemingly sense-less suffering? Dr. Van Impe explains from a bibli-

cal perspective why even Christians suffer and the best way to make the most of misfortune.

The Happy Home: Child Rearing
Many parents are confused about how to raise their children to love and serve God. Dr. Van Impe provides sound Bible principles, as well as practical advice for raising children to be happy Christian adults.

The Judgment Seat of Christ
Sheds light on the misunderstood subject of God's judgment. Covers the five judgments of the Bible, including the judgment of works, and a special section on the believer's crowns to be awarded on Judgment Day.

Religious Reprobates and Saved Sinners
A timely message by Dr. Van Impe that distinguishes "religion" from genuine salvation. If you've ever wondered how to separate the wolves from the sheep, you must read this frank, tell-it-like-it-is booklet!

This Is Christianity
Millions who claim to be Christians, including church members, are not because they have never been born again. The message of this book will help you understand this vital subject and know what it means to be a follower of Christ.

The True Gospel
The only "good news" is that Christ died for our sins, was buried, and rose again. There is no other good news. Dr. Van Impe also covers Christ's last

seven sayings upon the cross, and the importance of His resurrection.

What Must I Do to Be Lost?
Are you trusting in the traditions of men, your church, your good works? All the doctrines of the church will not get you into heaven. There is only one way to be saved—find out how in the pages of this book.

Order from:
    Jack Van Impe Ministries
    P.O. Box 7004 • Troy, Michigan 48007

In Canada:
    Box 1717, Postal Station A,
    Windsor, Ontario N9A 6Y1